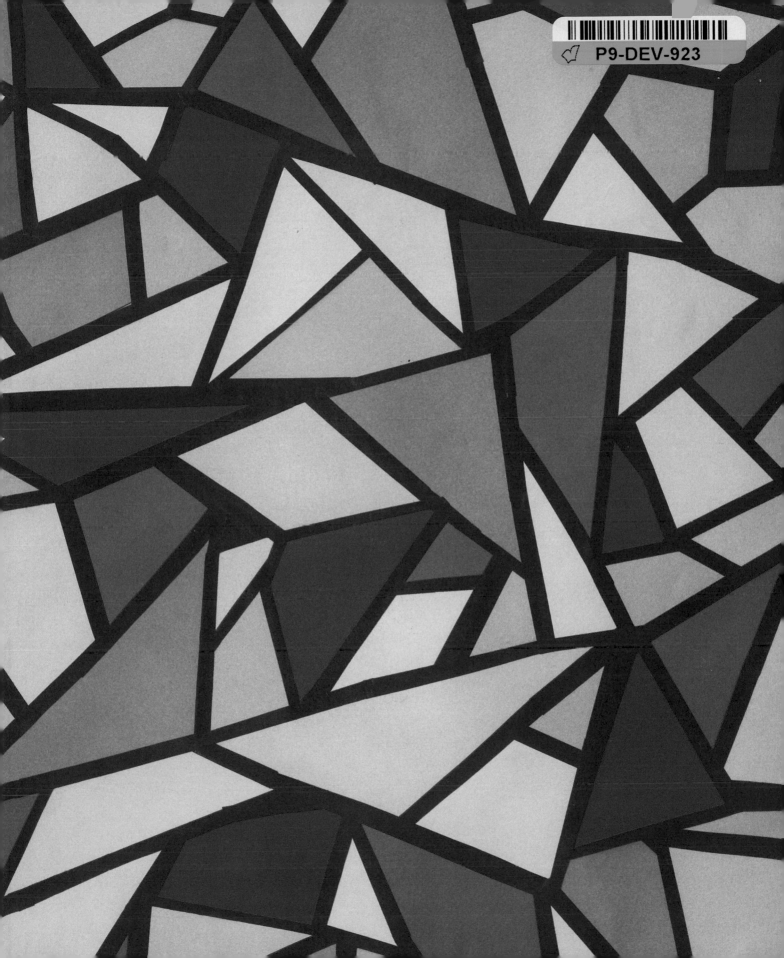

Simple Times

Simple times of yonder floating through my yesteryear.

The five & dime, an old church chime, simple times held dear.

Creaky wooden porch swings, main street marching bands,

Ice cream shops, thick muttonchops, and as always Grandma's hands.

A wizened chaotic tangle of stiff and knotted joints

Gnarledly curled, not quite unfurled, as she tries to point.

There is a simple tale to be told by Grandma's hands.

Worm-like veins don't speak in vain of all the years they've spanned.

Shakily scooping ice cream from cardboard carton gallons,

Frail and brittle, twistedly little, are these feeble talons.

When being clutched by Grandma's claw, I feel no need to convince her

The simple times, conveyed in rhymes, by her cold and boney pincer.

—Gene Woodchuck

Simple Times

written by

Amy Sedaris

and

Paul Dinello

GRAND CENTRAL
PUBLISHING

NEW YORK   BOSTON

Grand Central Publishing
Hachette Book Group
237 Park Avenue
New York, NY 10017
www.HachetteBookGroup.com

Printed in the United States of America

First Edition: November 2010
10 9 8 7 6 5 4 3 2 1

Grand Central Publishing is a division
of Hachette Book Group, Inc.

The Grand Central Publishing name and logo
is a trademark of Hachette Book Group, Inc.

Library of Congress Control Number: 2010928185
ISBN: 978-0-446-55703-0

Designed by Lenny Naar

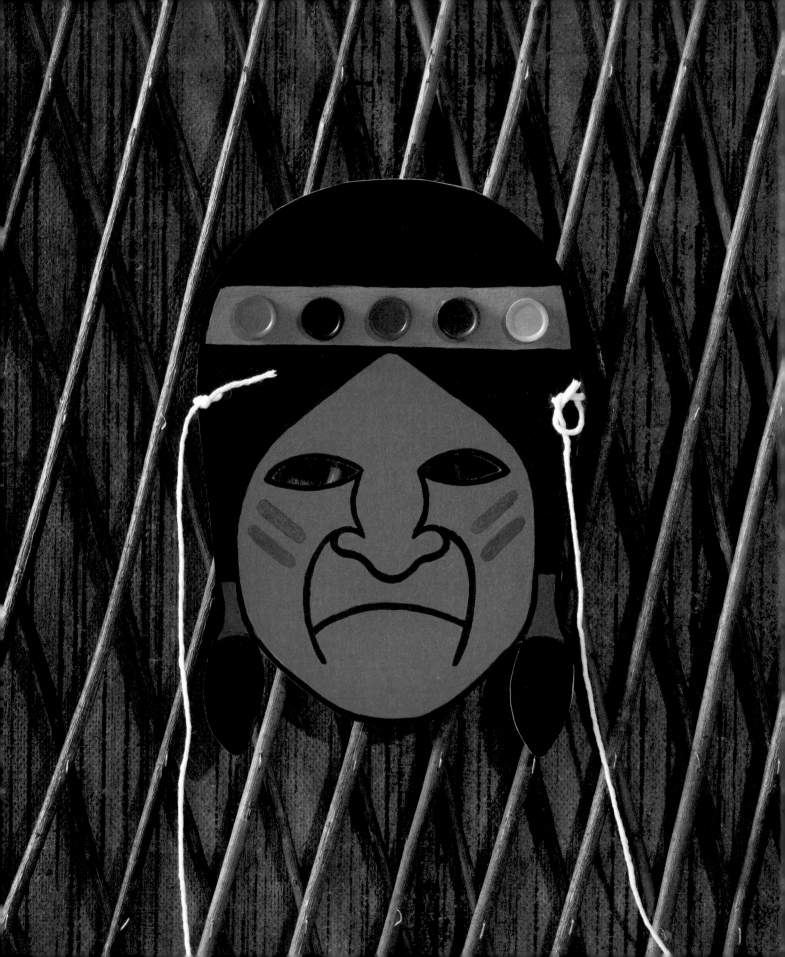

photography
by Jason Frank
Rothenberg

Embroidery Art
Megan
by
Whitmarsh

Illustrations by
Justin Heroux

Co-Art Direction
& Costume Design
by Adam Selman

Table of Contents

Hello, fellow crafters! What a wonderful opportunity for us to get to know each other, but be forewarned, this will be the only opportunity, because after this introduction, there will be little time for frivolous cordialities. It's going to be all about cutting, gluing, and hammering. So let's take a moment now, shall we? Obviously you know me, my name is stitched on the cover. Still unsure? Perhaps this will help: I am the adorable best-selling author of the thoughtfully hard-hitting tome on hospitality, *I Like You*. I'm guessing that information has cleared some cobwebs. As for me knowing you, why don't we make things easy, and call you "Twinkles." So, Twinkles, what's all this then about me writing more books when we both know I should be resting on my laurels? Well, after I changed the way the world entertains, I figured why not do the same for crafting?

It's often been said that ugly people craft and attractive people have sex. This book is not going to dispel that ridiculous fact. Rather, it will accept the well-documented, scientifically sound research done on the subject and move on, because regardless of how you look, this book is not here to judge, it is about the joy of crafting!

Crafting, or "making things," has always been a delightful pastime of mine because it requires putting common elements together in order to achieve a lovely something that nobody needs. But is it okay to make things?

It's natural for humans to suppress urges, for when our desires are left unchecked they lead to broken relationships, prison time, and forest fires. But there is one urge that should always be encouraged to blossom — the creative urge! Yes, it is healthy to want to make things, but that desire without guidance can lead to foreclosure, incest, and forest fires. Too often instruction for crafting is gutter-learned. Convoluted half-baked lessons picked up from street corners, back alleys, and scouting. *Simple Times* will provide crafters with the proper guidance, much like a parole officer. But this book is much more than a supervisor for crafting offenders; hopefully it will also inspire you, helping to spark or trigger new creative thoughts leading to a vast array of hastily constructed obscure d'arts.

Although this book is marketed toward sane, intelligent adults — frankly, that's where the money is — should it fall into the hands of the mentally challenged, it will do them no harm. Conversely, it will speak to them directly, addressing their special needs. For any educated, well-adjusted adult can glue Popsicle sticks together to create a cold plate trivet, but try the same simple task while hampered by a defective brain, and you will understand the full breadth of crafting.

This book includes an infinite* assortment of projects that utilize a wide range of skills and are inspired by many cultures, spanning from a Mexican Knife Sheath to a Mexican Sombrero. But most importantly, these projects will engage everybody: the sane, the not so sane, those hobbled with disabilities, those on the lam — anybody who's looking for a simple, creative way to kill a lot of time. And let's face it, we all have some time that needs to be killed.

Sincerely,

Amy SEDARIS

*actual number of projects determined by amount
 of space and author's level of fatigue

THE WHOS AND WHATS of CRAFTING

What Is Crafting?

Crafting includes a whole host of activities associated with skillful attempts at making useful things with your hands and resulting in stocking stuffers, grab bag items, and painted rocks. Some crafts have been practiced for centuries. These crafts were created using skills passed down from generation to generation, and were motivated by necessity, such as baskets and pottery, or artistic expression, such as more baskets and more pottery. Today, there is a much more leisurely attitude toward crafting, and virtually anyone without a job and access to pipe cleaners can join the elite society of crafters.

Is Crafting Right for Me?

Anyone can craft! There are an exhausting amount of crafts requiring a wide array of skills, so that regardless of age or artistic ability, there is a project that is perfect for you...if you possess the right natural tools. Unfortunately if you don't, all the desire, knowledge of cross-stitching, and yarn in the world will at best amount to hamster bedding. The following characteristics are essential for a successful crafter. Firstly, every crafter must possess a contortionist-like dexterity or monkey-hands, and strong agile fingers capable of bending thick wire into tiny intricate shapes, as well as a superhuman ability to clutch. Secondly, superior hand-eye coordination is critical. All crafters must excel at precise high-velocity hand movements not unlike the jaws of a snapping turtle or a lizard's tongue, if that lizard could decoupage with the same agility he uses to catch flies. Thirdly, it's important for all crafters to possess an inhuman tolerance for highly toxic chemicals. So, as you can see, crafting is an equal opportunity pastime; all are welcome as long as you fit the profile.

Ideas: Where Do They Come From?

Crafting is putting ideas into action and then holding them together with an inexpensive adhesive. But where do the ideas come from? Is it okay to wonder? Usually, the best ideas come from other people's good ideas, which then, after a short gestation period, become your ideas. But what if your friends are out of ideas? In that horrifying scenario you will be forced to think up your own ideas. It has been said that the more you use your imagination the more it will grow. Of course, that is much easier to say than to prove scientifically. I am often asked why I never run out of ideas and I always reply, "Do you think I'm pretty?" I may never know the answer to that question, but here are some things I do know: animals love snacks; clams don't have heads; never remove your own braces; and everything I see and hear gives me inspiration. Some people might walk by an old piece of furniture resting on the curb waiting for the trash men to haul away and all they see is a beat-up sofa. Do you know what I see? A couch, a place to sit or lounge, something to put cushions on, a settee, a couch, something that would go inside a living room. Imagination! My problem is that I have so many ideas, I never have enough time to use them all. Just the other day I thought up eleven things I could do with a flowerpot. Eleven! Three of those things didn't even involve plants. Imagination! Remember when the Cowardly Lion makes his crown out of a clay pot? That's one for me! Now it's your turn! Exercise your imagination muscle! How many uses can you come up with for

a flowerpot? Write down your answers. But don't write them in this book. Grab a separate sheet of paper. I didn't spend two and a half weeks writing a book just so you could mark up the pages with your silly ideas for things you can do with a flowerpot. When it comes down to it, what's wrong with a flowerpot just being a flowerpot? Why is nothing ever good enough for you?!

There are hundreds of dozens of ways to stimulate your brain so that the creative juices flow. Rummage through a Dumpster. Look at old album covers. Spend time at a Renaissance fair. Find new friends who have better ideas than your old friends. Explore garage sales and swap meets. Go crabbing! Buy fruit and let it get old. What shapes does it turn into? What kind of bugs does it attract? If you have a notebook and pencil, head over to the shopping mall. Record the items that are on display. Think about how you might alter them. What would glitter look like in that fish tank? How would shells look glued to that toilet seat? Let your mind wander, awash in possibilities. Imagine that luggage covered in beads! What items attract your attention? What things do you find appealing? Once your mind is stimulated you might feel you are ready to begin crafting, but not so fast. Where are you going to craft?

Creating a Craft Room

Having an attractively organized craft room increases efficiency and quality in your crafting. You will find that not only is a well-ordered workroom a pleasure to craft in, but it is also a magnet for young children. What with the myriad colors and sparkly objects on display, don't be surprised if a child wants to spend all day in there, which is unfortunate, because a craft room is the most dangerous room in the house! Even the most experienced crafters are often overtaken by fumes or fall victim to any number of objects that can slice, prick, or adhere.

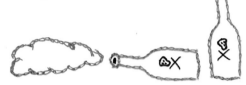

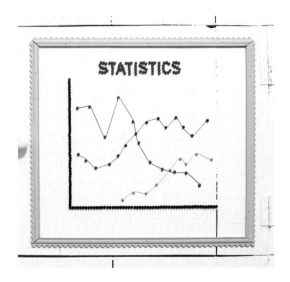

Crafting Statistics

MOST POPULAR CRAFTS

1 Tuna Can Lid Baby's Sleep Chime

2 Mr. Wiggly Worm

3 Macramé Pinch Pots

4 Crab Claw Roach Clip

5 Toilet Paper Roll Pirate

6 Seaweed Lampshade

7 Googly-eyed Clamshells

WHO IN THE WORLD IS CRAFTING?

More than 8 out of 10 households have at least 4 out of 5 family members engaging in 2 out of 3 crafts 78% of the time. A staggering 98% of this group are homosexual men.

HOW ARE WE USING OUR CRAFTS?

1 Camper decorations

2 Old people presents

3 Chew toy

4 Dust accumulator

5 As evidence that we don't spend all our time doing absolutely nothing

6 Salvaged for parts to make other crafts

MOST COMMON CRAFTING ACCIDENTS

1 Sawdust fires

2 Pinecone lodged in throat

3 Decoupage fatigue blackout

4 Dried flower fungal infections

5 Seed sensitivity

6 Hanged from a yarn noose

7 Feather asphyxia

8 Vaginal bleeding

When creating your craft room, the most important consideration is good ventilation. It's a shame that the most attractive crafts always raise the most hazardous dust or emit the most toxic fumes while being constructed. Anyone breathing this air, or being breathed on by someone who has been breathing this air, risks serious injury to his or her, but mostly her, health. What is meant by "ventilation"? Do you have a window in your workroom? If so, can you open it? Will it stay open by itself, or do you need to wedge a soup can in the opening? Do you get a cross breeze? Even with an open door and an operable window, this may not be adequate ventilation. Make a quick analysis of the room. Do you need all these walls? If so, how would one wall look with a three-by-four-foot hole torn in it?

Easy accessibility to materials is also key when putting together a craft room. All the items you need should be within reach. Do you have easy access to the scissors and the thread? Are the buttons at arm's length? How about the fire extinguisher and the respirator mask?

Nothing ruins a lazy afternoon of crafting quite like being struck by a cottonmouth snake. Be sure to line the baseboards of your craft room with professional grade snake snares.

Stocking your craft room with a variety of supplies is important for a fulfilling crafting experience. It is always helpful to have the right tool for the right job. For example, one might be attempting to adhere a fuzzy doodad to a frilly whatsit or a ruffled gewgaw to a tasseled thingy.

Using the incorrect glue in this situation can have tragic consequences. You will want to have a wide assortment of glues to choose from. But which is the correct glue to use in what situation?

Simple Glue Guide

Use Tacky with Furry, Gummy with Gritty, Paste with Prickly, and always Gloppy with Sandy. When working with Silky go Sticky, Smooth with Treacly and for everything else use a heavy-duty, industrial-strength epoxy.

Putting materials in either clear glass or well-labeled storage jars is a helpful idea. With just a glance you can immediately identify your materials so that the next time you need a pixie straw, you will not inadvertently reach for the can of utility knives, causing a lifelong facial disfiguration that haunts your crafting circle for years to come.

I personally find that having a bulky rug in a craft room is a mistake. It will become a haven for dropped pins, needles, and blades, turning the once comforting deep pile into a Viet Cong–style booby trap.

To sum up, when designing your craft room, plan an organized, well-ventilated area properly outfitted to protect from poisonous snake attacks.

Crafting for Profit or Turning Your Pompon Ringworm into a Cash Cow

Crafting for joy is its own reward, but unfortunately not a reward that pays the bills. It is only natural to behave as if your hobby is solely an act of passion, but on a deeper level, secretly hope that you can attain real power from it. This is also true for those who practice martial arts or act in community theater productions. If you want to create a craft that is a guaranteed moneymaker, here are a couple of simple, surefire ways to achieve it:

1 Make something that doesn't exist and nobody has ever thought of or even dared to dream about. An object so exceptional that it cannot be described by words because there is nothing of this earth to compare it to.

2 Start a fad or a trend. Create a craft item that immediately causes, on at least six of the seven continents, an unchecked fanaticism, especially connecting with the youth crowd.

But even if your ambitions are more moderate, there are a few simple characteristics your crafty handiworks should possess in order for them to create a subtle profit margin:

A. SUGGESTION OF DURABILITY

Does your project appear to the untrained eye to be of high quality? Will your project hold together on the shelf until it sells? Will it withstand the rigors of the shopper's scrutiny? Can it be bagged by an apathetic teenager with long, curly fingernails or an ex-convict on work release without coming apart? Remember, when you are applying the coffee bean to the pumpkin seed to the gourd, are you using enough glue for it to sustain the bumpy ride in the cart through the parking lot on its way to the trunk?

B. IRRESISTIBILITY

Does your project have that certain special something? What makes baby chicks and bunnies so adorable? Is it a magical quality? No. These adorable elements can be quantified and, more importantly, reproduced into a craft that can then be put up for sale. Let's break down the elements…

1 **Convenient size:** Chicks and bunnies are small enough to fit in your pocket or underpants drawer. People enjoy small things because they make them feel powerful and in control. It feels good to understand that in terms of the bunnies stuffed into your jeans, you are judge, jury, and executioner.

2 **Texture:** Chicks and bunnies are soft and furry, and people generally like soft, warm, and furry things. That is another reason it is so tempting to stuff them in your pockets.

3 **Eyes:** Humans are drawn to eyes. We find comfort there. Traditionally we don't have warm feelings for things that can't look back at us. When was the last time you cared for a rock or a log? Nobody has a special relationship with a stop sign, but stick a couple of eyes on it and suddenly it's a pleasure to yield. Peanut shells are often thought of as the barrier to the tasty nutmeat, and are commonly discarded. But once you can look that peanut shell in the eye, you will quickly realize you've found a nutty new friend: Hello, Sheldon, welcome to our home.

C. USEFULNESS

Don't worry about this one.

Doing what we love should be motivation enough for doing it, but there is nothing wrong with trying to make a fast buck off something that takes so little time and effort to achieve.

Jean Woodchuck   GENE WOODCHUCK

A Quick Note from the
Woodchucks

We are Gene and Jean Woodchuck, and we are the handy hints folks. That's not our official title, never asked to be called that, won't find it on a sign, and we don't have any formal training to back it up, but that's just the way it is. I guess it's just in our genes. We have been asked to take a look-see through this heap of pages and when the urge strikes, throw our two cents in. No big deal, don't want to make a meal out of it, nothing to write home about, just want to pass on a little bit of our know-how. We will be talking about useful crafty things such as: using a quality brush, the best way to organize your beads, and how to repair a wedding portrait that's been torn to shreds.

Although we are husband and wife, one type of advice we never give is relationship. Let's just say it's not our area of expertise. Look, everybody knows we've had our share of ups and downs. It's common knowledge. Don't need to dig it up again. It's well known that if you decide to walk by our place pretty much any time of day or night, you're gonna hear screaming and even though it might sound like a couple of hyenas fighting over a zebra carcass, we can pretty much guarantee that in between the words that can't be reprinted here, you're gonna hear a useful tip or two. That's just the way we are.

So what makes us such an authority on handy information? Trial and error. You see, we've been failing at simple home improvements and crafty projects for so long that there isn't an activity that we haven't screwed up, sometimes with some pretty costly results. Let me tell you something, you don't have to lose a lot of nephews before you figure out how to build a woodshed right. Yes we have our battle scars, yes there are lawsuits pending, and yes we are not allowed to legally operate in the state of Missouri, but that's what makes us experts.

So that's it. Every once and a bit, one of us will lob in a nugget of tip. If you can use it, fine. If not, that's no skin off our grafts. That ain't gonna change what we do. We're the Woodchucks, and we're just here to help, or not.

"it's in our genes!"

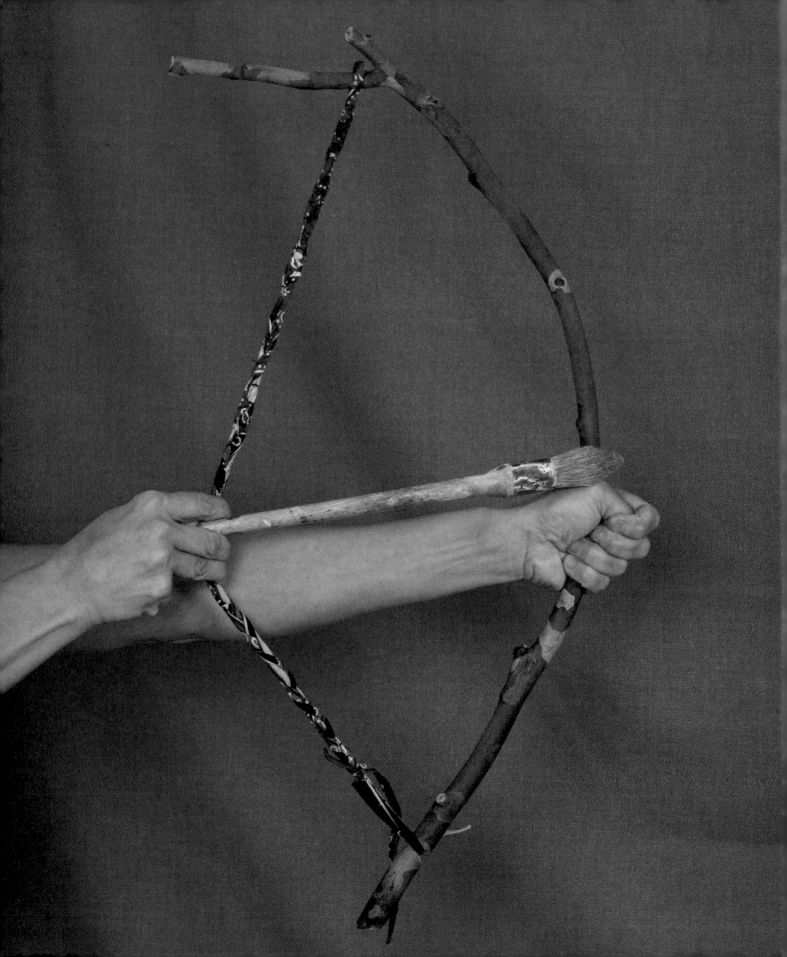

(The Craft of Crafting Craftingly)

Craft Yourself Homely

Remember the simple times? Ah, yesteryear, when simple was as easy as going home, and home was as simple as handwoven bread, homespun rocking chairs, oven-baked slippers, butter-churned pillow shams, and embroidered patchwork crisps.

Today when we think of "home," it's difficult not to conjure up such soulless phrases as "factory-blown prefabricated construction module," or "precut semi-structural drywall panel." Those words make us feel uneasy. It's difficult to get cozy in any environment that is "factory blown." Who doesn't long for the good old days when the structure you lived in was assembled by hand, hastily cobbled together using mud, hay, and horse urine, and "hominess" was as simple to obtain as consumption? But, even in the most sterile machine-made environment you can still acquire that "homemade" feel with the art of crafting. Warm and fuzzy is only a sock monkey away.

But what do we mean by "hominess," and why is it important? Although there is only one question mark at the end of that sentence, there are actually two questions in there. Let's tackle the first one. "Hominess" means comfortable and cozy, and it calls to mind traditional peasant life, when tools and utensils, furnishings, and adornments were all made by hand. It is that old-world charm that hominess embodies, a throwback to a charmingly simpler time, minus the unimaginably high infant mortality rate.

A warm nostalgia for what we feel comfort in pretending were the good old days.

As for the second question, the answer is simple. Handicrafting keeps us in touch with our roots. It reminds us that we are born of the natural world and that is where we shall return. Machine-made production removes humans from the process and once humans are removed, it is only a short step away from bands of flesh-eating robots ruling the night.

So the next time you turn on a fire in your fireplace by thoughtlessly flipping a light switch, give pause and remember Grandma and Grandpa, and what having a fire meant to them. Together they would trudge through waist-high snow, Grandpa lugging his heavy axe, and Grandma a pot full of her famous twig soup. After five or six hours hacking away at a tree and fighting off the brutal cold, they'd drag the heavy logs back to the porch. Grandma would prepare the wood by scouring each log against her washboard, while Grandpa tended to his chop wounds. And then, as dusk finally settled in, they'd sit side by side in their rocking chairs as the orange flames flickered, and they'd think silently to themselves, "God, I hope we don't have another chimney fire." And that is, at its core, what crafting is all about: finding a way back to a time of holding hands and ice cream pie, handmade rugs, and twice-baked rye, home again to simple times.

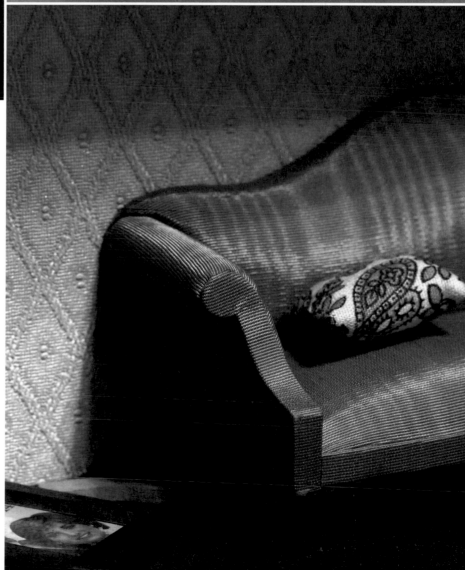

SANDPAPER RUG

Instructions: Cut a desired rug shape out of sandpaper. Color the shape with crayons, as this will make it appear to be a woolly rug.

DOLLHOUSE SHOWER CURTAIN

Instructions: Out of your favorite shower cap cut a 4 x 7-inch section. (During future showers, expect greatly reduced reliability from this cap.) Cut a 4-inch rod to hang the curtain on from a metal clothes hanger. Attach it with tiny jump rings.

DOLL WIGS AS DOORKNOBS

Instructions: When you feel you are too old to play with dolls, or more importantly, society does, there is a creative adult way to continue your relationship. Remove a doll's wig and place it over a doorknob, creating a festive furry handgrip. Also, you can remove the wig, and attach an elastic band and wear it as a beard or bangs. Instant new look.

HAIR LAMP

Instructions: During the 18th and 19th centuries, it was common to make jewelry or flowers out of hair as a moving memorial to a loved one. We hung hair swatches, culled by salons from anonymous heads, on a lampshade. Sew swatches onto lampshade or use jump rings, allowing the swatches to move more freely. Still, oddly moving.

OLDEN TYMEN STOVE

OWL MATCHSTICK HOLDER

Instructions: Cut out a silhouette of an owl from heavy black paper. Cover the outside of a matchbook in black paper and glue to the center of the owl cutout. Cut 1 inch off the top of the inside matchbox. Glue this box inside the...you've probably got it from here—if not, you have no business attempting this craft.

PENNY SPLITS-A-LOT (SEE PAGE 286)

Pays for itself!

Instructions: Sew a rag doll with freakishly long legs. Together the legs should be as long as the width of a door. Fill the legs with pennies. Place the doll with its legs split at the bottom of the door to block drafts. Excellent craft for smokers and shut-ins because it keeps smells from escaping.

NATIVE MASK

Folksy wall hangings will make any home more simple.

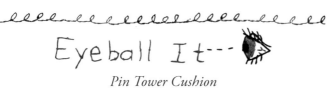

Eyeball It---

Pin Tower Cushion

SIMPLE TIMES PROTECTOR ROD

Protect your yesterdays from the uncivil tomorrows today! Don't delay.

Instructions: Saw the base off a broom, cutting the bristly sweeping mechanism free, and leaving only the handle. Decorate according to your personal sense of style. Place in window diagonally.

GENE'S CORNER

For my money, nothing makes the ole homeysteadier feel more homey than taxidermy. What with the way I drive, we get plenty of roadkill up here. It's almost like carcasses are falling out of the sky. When the wife's away, I like to spend most of my quality time in the stuffin' shed sewing up the pelts of my furry buddies and then displaying them on our bedside table. They are the first thing I see in the morning and the last thing I see before I shut the peepers, and guess what, other than me they are the liveliest thing in the room. Are you listening, Jean?

SEQUINED PILLOW

Instructions: Make a pillow out of muslin, any shape or size. Create shapes on pillow front using sequined trimming. When you are happy with the design, stitch the trimming to the pillow. Simple.

THUMBTACK FUNTACK

Instructions: Using a pencil, write a word on a piece of hardwood and then follow the lines using thumbtacks. You will need a thimble and a lady hammer because without them, over time this repetitive pressing will destroy your thumbs.

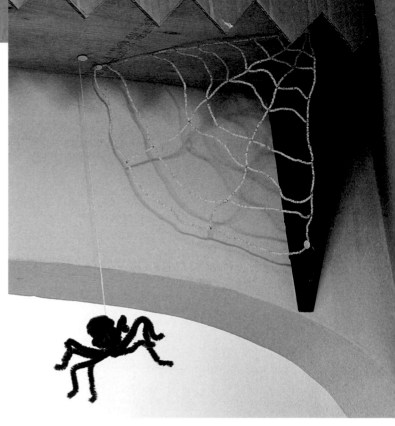

Jean's Quick Tip

Old hairnets make terrific spiderwebs!

FLOUR TORTILLA MIRROR

Instructions: Cut the center out of a doily. Run a basting stitch around the edge of the hole. This can be achieved by hand or with a sewing machine, you decide. But remember, simple times. I know you will make the right choice. Gather the center hole until it covers the edges of the mirror and has the desired amount of fullness. Mix 1 part white glue with 2 parts water. Either paint the mixture onto the doily or soak it in a bowl of the mixture and wring out the excess. Place the wet doily on a warm surface, such as a radiator, in the desired shape and let it dry. Hot glue to the mirror. To make mirror, cover the cardboard shape of a mirror with tinfoil.

BEADED SPIDERWEB

Instructions: Bead an intricately beautiful spiderweb. Once the web is complete, cut any pattern you like out of cardboard to use as shelf trimming.

POPSICLE STICK TRIVET (SEE PAGE 113)

Instructions: Using a sharp object, poke holes at the bottom and middle of each Popsicle stick. Put a bead in between each Popsicle stick while running wire through each hole to connect the sticks. Pull wire taut and secure while sticks are lying in a circular shape on a flat surface.

Money $ Saver

When stocking up on sticks for all your Popsicle stick crafts, purchase Popsicles in the winter, when they are cheapest, and let them defrost in your sink. Pressing on the white bag covers, determine if the contents feel liquid. If so, pull sticks out. The stained sticks will look more authentic. If you buy sticks free of frozen confectionery use cranberry sauce left over from the holidays to stain them.

35

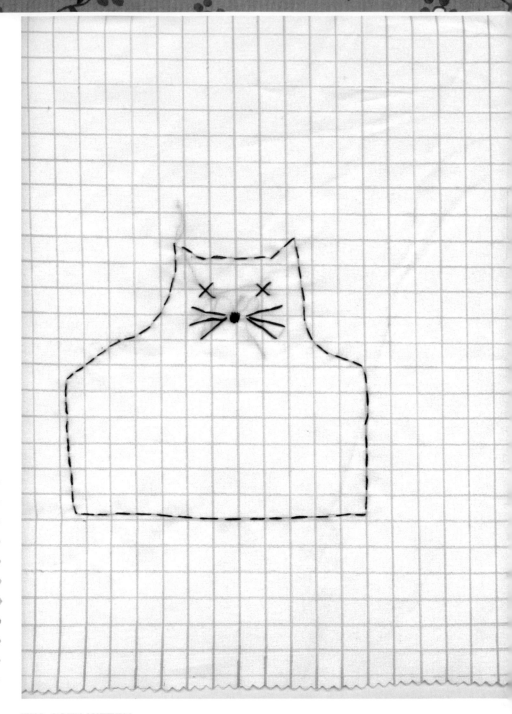

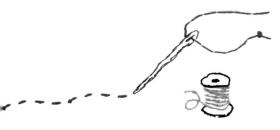

TEA COZY KITTEN

Instructions: Self-explanatory.

To make a puuurfect pot of tea, boil water and pour into an animal teapot figure. Add tea. Cover with handmade Tea Cozy Kitten. (Pattern included.)

Note: If teapots are not in constant use, place lumps of sugar in them and they will not have that musty taste guests comment about so often.

Craft Yourself Homely

PAPER TOWEL HOLDER
Materials: Spools!

LESLIE'S RUG
Costs peanuts!

Instructions: Use scrap fabric from dance costumes, left-behind garments from roommates past, and quilt fabric (from when you thought you had the patience to make a quilt). The fabric is wrapped around 100 feet of polypropylene rope, then zigzag stitched together. Think you can do better? Then make your own.

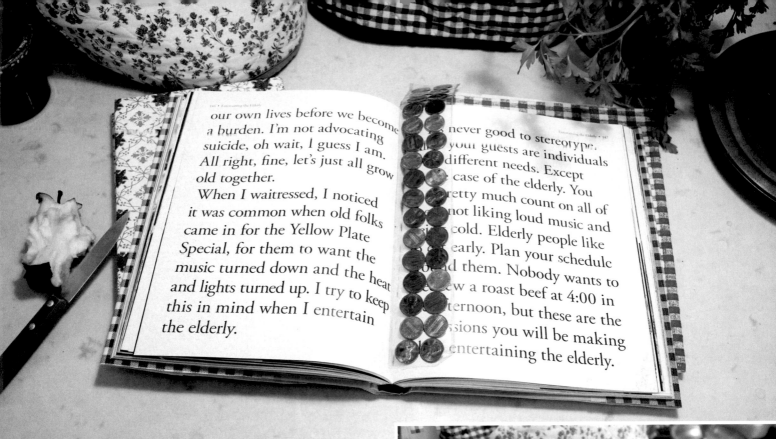

our own lives before we become a burden. I'm not advocating suicide, oh wait, I guess I am. All right, fine, let's just all grow old together.

When I waitressed, I noticed it was common when old folks came in for the Yellow Plate Special, for them to want the music turned down and the heat and lights turned up. I try to keep this in mind when I entertain the elderly.

never good to stereotype. your guests are individuals different needs. Except case of the elderly. You pretty much count on all of not liking loud music and cold. Elderly people like early. Plan your schedule them. Nobody wants to a roast beef at 4:00 in afternoon, but these are the ssions you will be making entertaining the elderly.

COOKBOOK COVERS

Instructions: Cut sections of vinyl tablecloth to use as covers for any book that has the potential to get stained on the job, such as a cookbook or a surgical manual.

BON.US CRAFT

PENNY BOOKMARK

Instructions: Sandwich 2 rows of pennies between 2 pieces of clear packing tape.

OVEN MITTS

Oven mitts come in handy.

LACY NAPKIN RINGS

Instructions: Cut a toilet paper tube into 3-inch rings. Cover the rings in lace or surgical gauze. Decorate the covered rings with ribbon or rickrack.

CRAFTY CANDLESTICKS!

Is there anything more pure and simple than a candle? Aside from its tragic history of catching kids' heads on fire during birthday celebrations and igniting Christmas trees, the candle can be a romantic and festive addition to most events. But unless you have a cadre of slave bees doing your bidding, keeping yourself in candles can become an expensive proposition, which is why it makes sense to make your own. Candles are relatively simple and fun to create, turning the chores of yesteryear into the hobbies of today.

DELIGHTFULLY CRAFTY CANDLESTICKS

Instructions: To make your Delightfully Crafty Candlesticks, use 2 drumsticks, each about 18 inches long. If you are going to purchase your drumsticks, ask the man at your local music store which sticks will give you the most bang for your buck, because some sticks are more expensive than others. Make sure that the candle stand you will be using is weighted, because 18 inches of wood tends to get top heavy. Sand the sticks so that the paint will apply more smoothly, but only sand up to the point that sits inside the candle stand. This will save you about an inch of paint. After each stick is painted in your own color choice, dip the tip in flaming red high-gloss paint to resemble a flame. Or as another bright idea, you can use glitter. It's that simple. *Note: These candles take at least 3 days to make but burn for a lifetime.*

Delightfully crafty candlestick
Less of a candle and more of a stick
No drippy wax, no sticky wick
All of the warmth with none of the flit
Delightfully crafty candlestick

To use as a votive is never the motive
Is it a taper? Only on paper.
No match to strike 'cause nothing is lit
You better believe it blows out quick
Delightfully crafty candlestick

During a blackout, don't you dismay
Although crafty candle won't light the way
If you survive till the night turns to day
You'll be greeted by crafty charming and gay
Adorable crafty candlestick, Yea!!!!!!!!!!
—Gene Woodchuck

CRAFTY CANDLE SALAD

Instructions: Place a lettuce leaf on your favorite plate or napkin. Stand several pineapple rings on top of the lettuce. Position half a banana in the hole of the pineapple. Top the banana with a smidgen of mayonnaise. Add a bright red cherry on top of the mayonnaise to resemble a burning flame for the Crafty Candle Salad.

Crafty Candle Salad

Pompon Hats

Buckles

Colonial Times

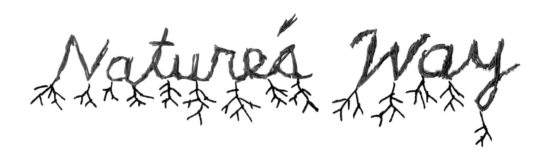

Nature's Way

What do an escaped convict, a lovable tramp, and an American Indian have in common? Aside from evading the law, the answer is crafting. They have a unique ability to construct from nature the items they need to survive, be it shelter, cooking implements, or picture frames made from twigs. But what is it about foraging in the wild that is conducive to crafting? The answer is simple: nature provides many raw elements that can be used to create, and, as loggers have so successfully shown us, they're all there for the taking. It's easy to criticize the raping of our natural resources, but clear-cutting is only one side of the equation: the other, less spoken about side is the charming semi-likeness of a spotted owl chiseled from a freshly chopped maple tree. Suddenly things seem a little more balanced. From seeds to nuts, leaves to twigs, rocks to pebbles, nature is a virtual craft store midnight madness sale. Need some dried straw to make a small basket? That bird's nest will do just fine. How 'bout a lampshade made from sticks? Why thank you, Mr. Beaver, for collecting them so neatly in that den-like pile. Nature has graciously provided all the elements; now it's up to you to assemble them and carry them away.

Bird feathers are a fantastic and simple way to ornament almost any project, but how do you go about capturing their plumage? Birds lose feathers when they molt, but finding them can sometimes prove to be time-consuming. Sometimes it's best to go right to the source. To obtain feathers from a bird, obtain a bird. Birds are often found by their nests, so those would be good places to stake out. If you find that birds are too elusive to get close enough to capture, you can always resort to using fear. Often birds frightened into flight will leave a few trophies. But sometimes the most efficient method of acquiring crafting resources requires marrying two seemingly useless items in nature—say a rock and a bird—so that they add up to something useful (in this case, feathers).

The riches of nature can be found everywhere, from protected marshlands to a stranger's backyard, but no place is more bountiful than her restless seas. Trolling through this soggy treasure trove you will find a myriad of living things in every shape and color. Shells, crustaceans, floating jungles of seaweed—nowhere else on earth has nature let herself go with such abandon quite like she has in her seas and sweeping beaches. It's as if Mother Nature threw a raucous party last night and then passed out before she could straighten up.

Often the most simple items in nature will make the most stunning crafts; for instance, colored stones. The list of things you can do with these faux gems is nearly endless, but I can only think of a couple. Searching for colorful stones can be as thrilling as digging for pirate's treasure, although you will find the thrill quickly diminishes once you realize what you're holding in your hand is a rock and not a Spanish doubloon. Rocks are a pleasing addition to any craft that is enhanced by something cold, hard, and often jagged.

What is most beautiful about nature is that it is bountiful and there is nobody around to put a price tag on it. So add nature crafts to your handicrafts repertoire because no matter how many shell necklaces you create, nature is always gonna make more mollusks, and if for some reason she doesn't, we can always go back to stringing packing peanuts for our handmade neck accoutrement needs.

ACORNS

- GATHER ACORNS IN THE FALL. LET THEM DRY ON TRAYS 1-2 MONTHS. THE CAPS WILL POP OFF THE NUTS. GLUE THE CAPS BACK ONTO THE NUTS.
- CUT A WREATH SHAPE OUT OF CARDBOARD OR JUST BUY A MASONITE RING AT THE CRAFT STORE
- GLUE THE ACORNS ONTO THE WREATH FORM

TOOLS
GLUE GUN   THICK CARDBOARD
ACORNS

BARK CONTAINERS

- COLLECT SOME FALLEN TREE BARK ON THE GROUND.
- APPLY GLUE TO TIN CAN AND WRAP BARK AROUND THE CAN HOLDING IT IN PLACE WITH RUBBER BANDS UNTIL IT DRYS
- CUT LID OUT OF BARK WITH SCISSORS

MATERIALS
BARK
GLUE
SCISSORS
RUBBER BANDS
TIN CAN

NUT CRAFT

NUTLY

flax

rye

thistle

wild rice

Japanese Maple

Honey Locust

Black Locust

mung bean

red bean

corn

pinto bean

black bean

navy bean

Cathy Camper Seed Art

MINT JULEPS

Instructions: Put a little water and a few spoons of sugar in a tall glass and stir to dissolve. Add several sprigs of fresh mint. Mash the mint in the sugar syrup against the glass with the spoon to get as much flavor out of the mint as possible (a long-handled spoon works best to get down to the bottom of the glass). Next is the hard part—crush ice in a towel with a mallet or the side of a hammer to get finely chipped ice (only freshly crushed works). You pretty much have to do two batches per glass. Fill the glasses to the top with crushed ice—no skimping—and then fill up the glass with bourbon (it fills quickly since there's not much room left after all the ice has been put in the glass). Insert a straw and stir to mix the mint and bourbon a little. Add a sprig of mint for decoration, and serve immediately.
Warning: They go down easily but can be very lethal.
Courtesy of Hugh Hamrick.

DONUT SQUIRREL FEEDER

Instructions: Squirrels love old-fashioned donuts. Use 2 metal jar lids that are roughly the size of an old-fashioned donut. Using a nail and hammer, make a hole in the center of each lid. Sandwich the donut between the 2 lids and run a string through the holes, making sure the string is knotted at one end. Hang so squirrels can enjoy!

NATURE'S CANDY

(raisins)

PEACE PIPE

Peace pipes or calumet pipes were traditionally smoked to seal treaties. Today pipes are smoked for a variety of reasons: if one is looking to "chill," to signify that one is "chillin'," or as a way to cement, between two parties, an agreement to "chill."

RED INDIAN MASK AND POMPON CORN

Quercus alba White Oak

SMOKIN' CRAFTY FIRE

Instructions: Paint 3 toilet paper rolls with marsh-brown paint. Once dry (or not, depending on your schedule), assemble like fire logs into a pile. Top with tissue paper of flame-like hues. Surround with small pebbles.

COCO'S TREE LORE

Aspirin comes from the aspen tree.

Beechnut gum is made from the beech tree.

The sweetgum tree is so named because pioneers
used its wood for toothpicks and toothbrushes.

The lower leaves on trees, searching for sunlight,
are always larger than the leaves on the top of the tree.

The sassafras tree is used to make root beer and
sarsaparilla.

HOW CAN WE IDENTIFY RED AND WHITE OAKS?

Johnny Stanley says:

"The Indian (red man) hunted with bow and arrow,
therefore oak leaves with pointed tips are red oaks. The
white man hunted with gun and bullet, therefore oak
leaves with round tips are white oaks."

53

PINECONE TOTE

Pinecones are adorable. So why, after collecting them from the forest floor, would you clumsily carry them by shoveling them into the pouch you made by cupping your T-shirt? Well, now you don't have to.

CATTAIL MAGIC

Instructions: Stick toothpicks in the bottom of miniature Chinese corncobs. Once impaled, roll the corn in a pile of cinnamon. Add leaves made from green construction paper.

DOODIE DUNGEON

Nothing is more inconvenient than having nature call you from her own backyard. Certainly, on the list of annoyances when outdoors, number two would be number one. Finding the appropriate place to "drop a deuce" while amongst the flora and fauna can prove to be troublesome. One might think that behind any random tree is an appropriate place to "build your log cabin," but unless you are immediately evacuating the area, you will quickly become aware of your faulty thinking by this fly-attracting, stench-producing nuisance. That is why the Doodie Dungeon is an essential.

Instructions: Away from air you might breathe, dig a 2 x 2-to-4 foot hole that is 4 feet deep. After each "consecration," cover with a thin layer of dirt. Bombs away!

BONUS 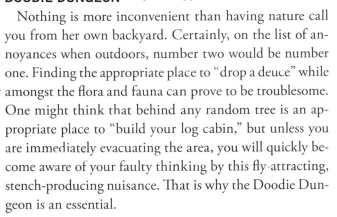 CRAFT

Sticks make excellent toilet-paper-roll holders. To keep roll dry, cover with a plastic bag, or drop the roll into a coffee can.

DRIED BEAN PODS (SEE PAGE 246)

Dried bean pods make wonderful instruments. Rattle when dry!

Knitted Outdoor Vest

Hot-on-the-Trail Moccasins

WORM BIN

HOW TO MAKE A WORM COMPOSTING BIN

Find a plastic storage container with a lid. It's best to salvage one rather than purchase a new container.

Drill a few holes in each side of the bin near the lid as well as several holes in the lid itself. These aerate the container and decrease any unpleasant odors. To avoid leakage and messes, do not drill holes near the bottom.

Get some red composting worms. To find worms, check your local arboretum or botanical garden, or call around to various greenhouses in your neighborhood. Gardeners are usually pretty nice, especially if you bring them weed in exchange for the worms.

Put your red worms in the bottom of your bin along with a little soil.

Place a few cups of kitchen scraps in the bottom of the bin, away from the worms, along with shredded paper. You can't overfeed worms but if there are too many scraps, the food will go uneaten, rot, and smell bad. The idea is for the worms to eat the scraps and leave behind their casings (waste or humus). The worm casings are excellent fertilizer for your plants and garden. Worms will only eat fruit and vegetable scraps. No meat, dairy, or baked goods should be used in your bin. Also, worms tend to like tomatoes, yams, and other sugary vegetables and fruits.

Fill the bin to the top with shredded paper. Water your bin as needed. Start with a cup or two. The bin should be "moist like a snack cake" but never muddy or sopping wet. The worms need to stay wet to be healthy.

Place the bin in a dark corner, underneath your sink or kitchen cabinets. Remember, your worms like to live in the dark.

When available, place your kitchen scraps in various corners of the bin, moving your worms around. This will make it easier to separate the casings when they're ready, since the worms migrate. Use the casings as needed. You can make a "tea" with the casings and use it to water your plants. The casings can also be mixed in with dirt to make a nutrient-rich potting soil.

Courtesy of Adam Ottavi Schiesl.

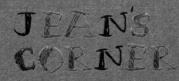

JEAN'S CORNER

Feeling down? Make a Self-Esteem Shell Collage! Write a poem on a piece of paper about you and the ocean and about how you feel about the ocean and why you are special and of course the ocean and then surround the poem with whatever shells you collected that day so you will always remember it. The best time to hunt for shells is after a storm. Hopefully, those times will coincide with the times you are feeling down.

To me, walking through the woods feels like watching a foreign film with subtitles. When watching those films, you miss so much because you're having to do all that extra reading; in the woods, you have to always look down to avoid vines that can trip you or snakes that can bite you, or snakes that look like vines trying to trip you, and then bite you. But I'll tell you this much: even more upsetting than snakes and vines, is running into a lazy camper. The woods is no place to cut corners. Right, Gene? Speaking of which, when I'm camping with a nut, I crave nuts. I like to save my empty walnut shells and string them up together to hang outside my tent. The sound of them clicking against one another puts me to sleep like nothing else.

SWEETGUM ART

Instructions: Collect a fistful of "gumballs" from the sweet-gum tree. Spray paint them gold. Also spray paint a multitude of toothpicks gold. Stick the toothpicks into the holes of the "gumballs," creating stars. Stack stars in unique configurations creating sculptures. Naturally simple.

STUFFED MUSHROOMS

36 baby portobello mushrooms,
   stems removed and
   finely chopped
4 scallions, chopped
1 pound Italian sausage
1 cup seasoned breadcrumbs
⅛ cup mayonnaise
½ cup Parmesan cheese

With a little butter, sauté mushroom stems and scallions. Add sausage and brown. Drain off fat and add ½ cup of the breadcrumbs and the mayonnaise. Mix well and stuff into the mushroom caps. Place caps in baking dish. Mix the remaining ½ cup of breadcrumbs with the Parmesan cheese and sprinkle on top of stuffed mushrooms. Bake 10–15 minutes at 450 degrees F, or until tops are browned.

As seen in *I Like You,* page 118.

ROCK RINGS
These gather no moss!

KILLING JAR
Instructions: The easiest way to kill your butterflies is to use a killing jar. Simply soak cotton balls in ethyl acetate and toss them into a jar along with the insect. A label on the jar makes the whole thing cuter.

WASHED UP JEWELRY
Instructions: Comb the shores of beaches in areas where residents come from "old money" for broken shards of china. Sand down the sharp edges and glue a pin to the back.

Painted Rocks

SHELL CRAFT

DROPOUT CRAB CLAW ROACH CLIP
Instructions: Save the claw from a crab, and hot glue a roach clip to the claw.

TURTLE SHELL MASK (SEE PHOTO ON PAGE 250)
Instructions: Paint a shell to look like a mask.

MOUTHWATERING CLAM CHOWDER
Clams! Exciting to catch, delicious to eat.
Instructions: To create the clams to accompany your tasty chowder, collect about a dozen hard-shell or cherrystone clams. Clean to remove salt and sand. Attach googly eyes right above the mouth opening. Enjoy until you hear a sound resembling a call for help.

SEASHELL CONCH SHELL NIGHT LIGHT
Here's a bright idea.
Best time to hunt for shells is after a storm.

COCONUTS!

(Pronounced "Co-Co-Nuts")

There are so many things you can do to a coconut, it's alarming that this large brown seed of the tropical palm has been so largely ignored.

It is true that coconuts are upsetting to work with. Their sturdy woody husks resist most attempts to be crafted, and, even when you are successful at breaching their fibrous skulls, they are prone to shatter. Not to mention the wispy hair-like strands that fly everywhere. So, are they worth it?

Look through this section of the book. When in your lifetime have you ever seen a coconut subjected to this type of treatment? Now you tell me if they're worth it.

Here are some shell-shocking coconut recipes and crafts that will enhance your home and workplace.

DAMN ITS

3 cups shredded coconut

1 cup sweetened condensed milk

⅛ teaspoon salt

1½ teaspoons pure vanilla extract

½ teaspoon pure almond extract

Mix all ingredients together. Make sure your cookie sheet is greased. Spoon drop a cat-paw-sized dollop of macaroons, press lightly, and bake in a 350-degree oven for 15 minutes.

Courtesy of Jennifer McCullen.

COCONUT PATTIES

1 teaspoon pure vanilla extract

½ cup sweetened condensed milk

3 cups shredded coconut

Mix all ingredients together and shape into small patties. Place on a greased cookie sheet and bake at 350 degrees F for about 18 minutes. Makes about 24.

Courtesy of Donny Mungus.

GENE'S CORNER

I love coconut crafts!

Nothing amuses me more than halfing a coconut and stringing the two pieces across my chest like women's breasts. But trust me, opening the shell of a coconut can present quite a challenge unless you know the proper technique.

1. Hold a coconut in the palm of your hand.
2. Notice that there are three "holes" at one end of the coconut. Two will have ridges that resemble eyebrows, and the third will look like a mouth that appears to be shrieking.
3. Tighten your grip on the coconut firmly so that it cannot get away, sticking your fingers forcefully into the "eyes," and covering the "mouth" as if to stifle a scream.
4. Using the blunt edge of a meat cleaver or hatchet, repeatedly strike the "forehead" of the coconut, continuing to pummel until you feel the "skull" crack and the coconut fluid seep from the battered "cranium."
5. Wash your tool, being especially careful to make sure the blade is free of any wisps of hair or coconut plasma and the handle has been wiped clean. Return it to its hiding spot.
6. Scrape out the coconut meat.

Start crafting!

Coconut Face Pin

LOAFING AROUND COCONUT HEAD CAKE

  3 cups cake flour, sifted

  3 teaspoons baking powder

  1 teaspoon salt

  ½ cup unsalted butter

  1½ cups sugar

  1 cup shredded coconut

  1 cup water

  1 teaspoon pure lemon extract

  4 egg whites, stiffly beaten

Sift together flour, baking powder, and salt. Set this aside. Cream the butter and the sugar and mix together until the mixture is fluffy. Add the coconut. Alternate adding the flour mixture and water, a small amount at a time. Beat until smooth.

Add lemon extract and fold in the egg whites.

Grease a 3 x 4 x 8-inch loaf pan and then pour in the batter, and bake in a 350 degree-oven for 1 hour and 15 minutes.

COCONUT FROSTING

  2 egg whites

  1½ cups sugar

  5 tablespoons ice water

  ¼ teaspoon cream of tartar

  1 teaspoon pure vanilla extract

  1¾ cups slightly sweetened coconut without coconut milk

  (comes in a tin)

Note: You will need a double boiler.

Put egg whites, sugar, water, and cream of tartar in the top part of the double boiler. Beat using a rotary egg beater until thoroughly mixed. Place over rapidly boiling water, beat constantly and cook for 7 minutes or until frosting stands in peaks. Remove from the flame. Add vanilla and ¾ cup of the coconut. Beat until thick enough to spread. Sprinkle the remaining 1 cup of coconut over the frosted loaf cake.

Courtesy of Donny Mungus.

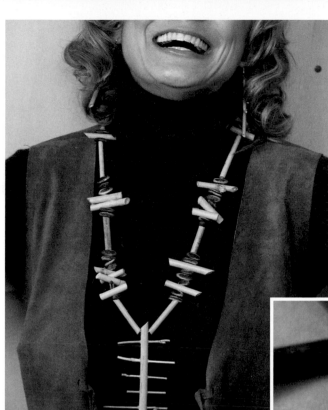

COCONUT CHIP NECKLACE AND BAMBOO EARRINGS

Instructions: To create exotic earrings, run a wire though a piece of coconut shell so that the razor-sharp shards dangle freely close to your face.

Warning: No hugging or swift head turns.

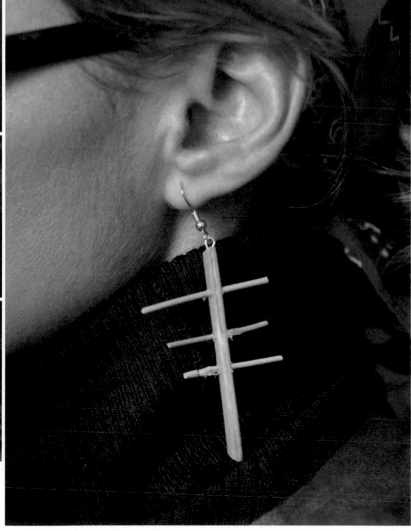

Toasting Coconut

TINTING COCONUT

Place some shredded coconut on a white piece of paper. Dilute a pinch of color paste in 1 teaspoon of water. Pour on top of the coconut and rub it through.

TOASTING COCONUT

Spread shredded coconut in frying pan on low heat and shuffle the flakes around using your fingers until the flakes look tanned.

Clothespins!

Matches!

The Joy of Poverty

Most sensible people look at poverty as an appalling condition in which one is deprived of even the most basic human needs, but do you know how I see it? A fortunate opportunity for creative resourcefulness. Whenever I take a little field trip to the rundown shacks of the most needy, I am always delightfully impressed by the inventiveness I see, such as the use of charmingly simple string to replace missing hardware on a well-worn dresser, or rubber from an inner tube to fashion a terrific makeshift door hinge. With the exception of the squalid living conditions, widespread humiliation, rampant disease, and the lack of quality meat, I envy the poor.

Our desperate ancestors used every scrap and tatter in a variety of ingenious ways. Nothing went to waste. Even an old stove was not left for the scrap heap. It was disassembled to make wind chimes, paperweights, and other kinds of weights and whatever was left over was woven into a quilt. Nothing was discarded. Even though we are amused by the abject poverty of our forebears, their spirit of making something out of nothing is one we should still embrace today. We can feel a sense of pride when we turn what most consider "garbage" into an eye-pleasing creation. It would be hard not to feel delight when a neighbor glares at your new front lawn black rubber flower planters, giving you the opportunity to say, "Believe it or not, those used to be tires!"

Each morning, after a long night's sleep upon my Queen Coil Plush-O-Pedic mattress, a breakfast of croque monsieur, and a full-body facial, I am faced with the daunting task of being creative for creative's sake. I don't have the benefit of pauperism. Being poor is a wonderful motivation to be creative, sort of a perennial carrot on a stick, but not an actual carrot because easy access to free food would only defeat the lucky stroke that is poverty.

Scrappy Bottle Cap Shoe Scraper

CUT-RATE HINGE

Instructions: Cut the shape of a hinge from an old rubber tire. If you have trouble finding a discarded tire, borrow one from a neighbor's car late at night. Nail the cut-out strip of tire to a door and frame, in place of the hinge. *Note: If using a neighbor's tire for this craft bury unused portion of tire, or place in another neighbor's garage.*

POOR MAN'S TOFFEE

Instructions: Place a can of unopened condensed milk in a pan of water and simmer for 2½ hours. Add water to the pot as the water boils down. After the 2½ hours, remove the can from the heat and let it cool. Open the can and eat right out of it. The "toffee" should be tan in color. To make this more attractive, remove the label from the can before simmering in the water.

THE UNABLE TO MAKE ENDS MEET BELT

Instructions: Roll a sheet of plastic wrap into a tight strand. Feed through the front two loops on your pants and tie in the front, pulling those loops closer together.

BUDGET TOOL RACK

Instructions: Find a good strong board at a neighbor's, but not the same neighbor you may or may not have borrowed a tire from. Nail 3-inch strips of rubber or leather onto the board, spaced a couple inches apart and leaving a bit of slack so that the tool handles will fit through the loops. Screw eye hooks into the top in order to hang the rack.

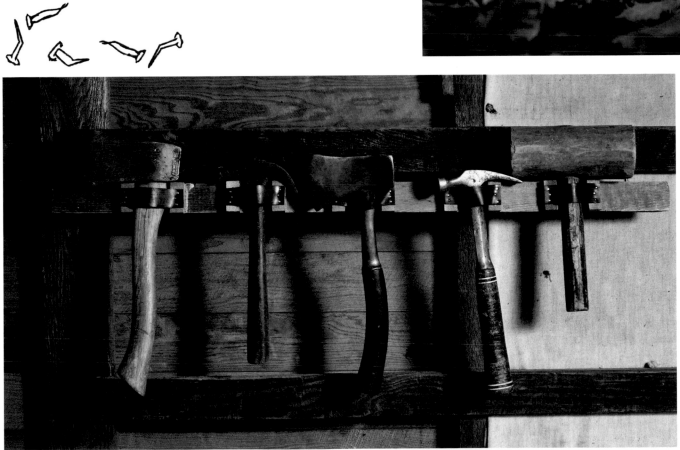

SHIRT BOX FRAME

I saw this idea in the movie *Equus*. A boy had a picture of a horse inside a shirt box that was hanging on his slanted wall. Shirt boxes make excellent picture frames: either paste a picture inside or paint right on it.

THE MAKE A WISHBONE SLINGSHOT

Instructions: Save the wishbone from a chicken or a turkey. Clean the meat off and dry out. Cover with colorful string. Attach two rubber bands to the wide ends of the bone after stringing them through a small strip of leather you have cut from the underside of a piece of furniture you no longer fancy.

JAILHOUSE BOX

Instructions: Toothpaste boxes make excellent pencil holders. Save or find two different-sized toothpaste boxes. Place the smaller one inside the larger one. Decorate the outside.

HOBO FIRE IN A CAN

Instructions: Place a roll of toilet paper in a coffee can, douse with rubbing alcohol, and ignite, unless this is your only roll of toilet paper. Then, under any circumstances, do not place in a coffee can and light on fire. This will keep you warm on a cold night.

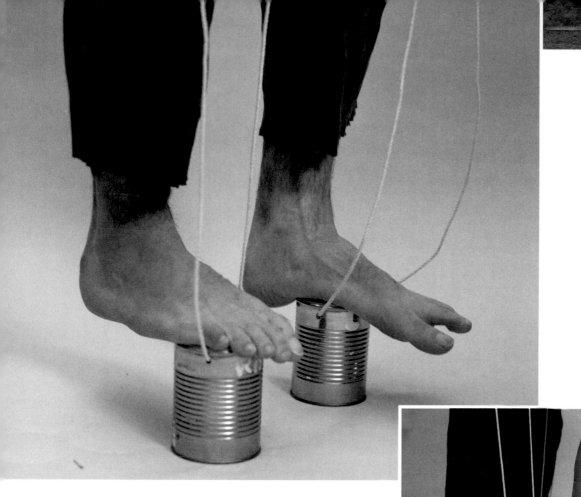

TIN CAN STILTS

Instructions: The bigger the hoof, the bigger the cans you will need. Remove the labels and drill 2 holes on either side toward the top of 2 tin cans. Run a sturdy string, about twice the length of your legs, through the holes. Make a handle using the cardboard from a clothes hanger.

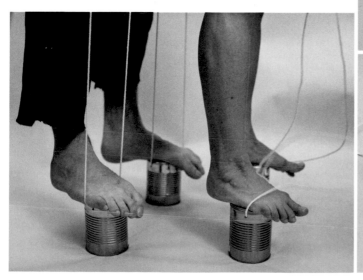

Trigger Ideas

Matchstick Frame and Needle Book

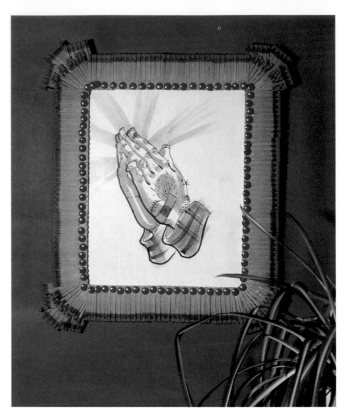

ROLLING THE DOUGH DICE

Instructions: Remove the crust from a slice of white bread and form what's left into small cubes. Leave out to dry, while occasionally re-moisturizing them with water. The final drying stages should take place in front of a fire. Use a marker to add the number dots once the dice are dry. Craps!

CUT-RATE SANDWICH BAG CONDOM

SARAN WRAP CONDOM.

ROPE DOLL

Instructions: Knot a rope in the shape of a human. Make a dress from fabric scraps and hair from old tights.

DRAWER DIVIDER

Instructions: Attach random boxes together using staples or tape. Line the insides of the boxes with an old vinyl tablecloth cut to fit.

GENE'S CORNER

The only way to end poverty is for those who got it to give to those who ain't. For instance, this spring I hired a couple of Mexicans to build a fence out of old bed frames around the below-ground pool pit I just dug. I guess there is some law or something, at least that's what my neighbor with the clumsy kid told me. Anyway, I'm not sure where these leather-faced tawny rascals came from and frankly I don't care—as far as I'm concerned they are hair-soot angels from heaven. They never complain, at least not in a language I can understand, they tote rocks like a mule, and I can practically pay them in cheap beer. I no longer remember the point to this story, so I'm gonna go for a dip before the pit dries up.

PUSH IT THROUGH DUSTER

Materials:
  8-inch-long scraps of fabric strips, as
  well as yarn
  1 clothes hanger

Instructions: Bend a wire clothes hanger into a "U" shape. Attach the pieces of fabric and yarn to the wire by looping them over and then pushing them through.

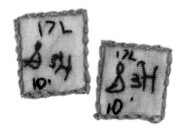

<u>Green Stamps</u>

Green stamps, green stamps
all over the floor
I cut and I snip
but always need more

My government cheese
melts on the sill
cuz my fridge got turned off
when I didn't pay the bill

My water is cold
and gotta keep the lights dim
my toilet is clogged
with rust on the rim

I sit on the bare mattress
as the sun comes up
stirring tap water into
my instant-coffee cup

Waiting for the day
that my number is called
hope my coffin is warm
and with money is walled

Cash I will need
cuz hell ain't cheap
but I'll live high on the hog
when I'm six feet deep

—Callie Thorne

GREEN STAMP KLEENEX BOX

Instructions: Cover a tissue box with unused green stamps, which are impossible to find because they don't give them out anymore. Secure with tape.

RATTLE BOXES

Instructions: Fill a box with random objects like bingo chips or jacks. Seal the box, cover it in fabric, and stitch around the edges.

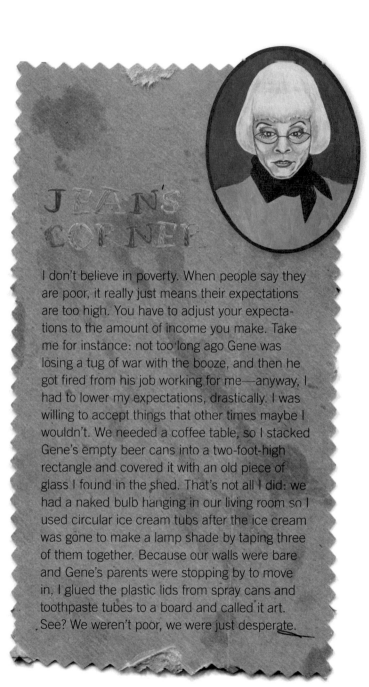

JEAN'S CORNER

I don't believe in poverty. When people say they are poor, it really just means their expectations are too high. You have to adjust your expectations to the amount of income you make. Take me for instance: not too long ago Gene was losing a tug of war with the booze, and then he got fired from his job working for me—anyway, I had to lower my expectations, drastically. I was willing to accept things that other times maybe I wouldn't. We needed a coffee table, so I stacked Gene's empty beer cans into a two-foot-high rectangle and covered it with an old piece of glass I found in the shed. That's not all I did: we had a naked bulb hanging in our living room so I used circular ice cream tubs after the ice cream was gone to make a lamp shade by taping three of them together. Because our walls were bare and Gene's parents were stopping by to move in, I glued the plastic lids from spray cans and toothpaste tubes to a board and called it art. See? We weren't poor, we were just desperate.

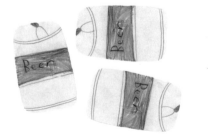

81

MILK CARTON SKID ROW

MILK CARTON HOUSE

MATERIALS

MILK CARTON Qt or HALF GAL. SIZE
X-ACTO BLADE
ELECTRIC CANDLE
NEWSPAPER
4 SHEETS BLANK NEWSPAPER 16" x 20"
1 SHEET WHITE TISSUE PAPER
WHEAT PASTE - 4 CUPS MIXED
BOWL, SPOON, 3 IN. PAINT BRUSH
STAPLER
LRG GARBAGE BAG TO COVER WORK AREA

DIRECTIONS

① WASH AND DRY MILK CARTON.

② OPEN UP THE TOP, STUFF WITH WADDED UP NEWSPAPER TILL PACKED.

③ STAPLE THE TOP CLOSED. BRUSH WHEAT PASTE ONTO CARTON AND WRAP IT IN FOUR LAYERS OF BLANK NEWS-PRINT, BRUSHING WHEAT PASTE ONTO EACH LAYER AS YOU GO, AND RUBBING WITH YOUR HANDS. ENCASE THE ENTIRE CARTON WITH PAPER AND PASTE. ALLOW TO DRY THOROUGHLY 2-3 DAYS.

④ USING AN X-ACTO BLADE, GET BUSY AND START CUTTING WINDOWS OUT OF YOUR NEW HOUSE

⑤ CUT OPEN THE BOTTOM OF THE HOUSE AND REMOVE ALL THE STUFFING.

⑥ BRUSH THIN LAYER OF WHEAT PASTE ON HOUSE AND WRAP 1 SHEET OF TISSUE PAPER AROUND THE HOUSE. LET DRY.

⑦ PLACE HOUSE OVER ELECTRIC CANDLE.

DO NOT LEAVE UNATTENDED, PROBABLY A FIRE HAZARD

MOUSE GHETTO

When a mouse has been injured in a trap or eaten poison and the end is near, there is something you can still do for him.

Create a mouse ghetto in which he can spend his final days feeling at home.

Materials:

A cardboard box

A Mouse Match-tress (see page 136)

Saltine crackers to use as canvases

Some tatters of things

Leftover soup and coffee grounds

Maybe some paint

The ability and desire to create a depressing space

Instructions: Create an environment of quiet despair by giving the mouse the vestigial remnants of his former life but reducing the colors and appointments to the bare minimum so as not to give him hope. Use coffee grounds to distress the mouse mattress.

After a while the mouse's life force will wither and you will have done your best, which is not good enough, to assist in the expected final outcome for which the mouse was most certainly headed.

The Joy of Poverty

RUSTY NAIL WIND CHIME

Instructions: Gather all the rusty nails in your backyard (see page 101). String them up using a strong, colorful string.

DECORATIVE FLY STRIPS

Instructions: Flies are attracted to stained glass, as evidenced by my experience of going to church. Surround a 6-inch-long strip of toupee tape with cardboard, creating a frame. Cut shapes out of the cardboard and cover with colored cellophane. You will find that this is both attractive and lethal, the best of both worlds.

Pennies

Coffee Filters

Handicraftable

There is absolutely no reason a handicapped crafter should abstain from crafting. The previous sentence is important so it shall be repeated. There is no reason, with the exception that the final results will range from inadequate to hilarious, that a handicapped crafter—socially, physically, or mentally—should abstain from crafting.

But what do we mean by handicapped anyway?

Defining disabilities is complicated, because they are relative to the culture in which they occur. For example, in many cultures, a double hand-severing might be perceived as a setback, but in mythical China, a man of means would close his fists, allowing his fingernails to grow into his palms and through to the other side, rendering his hands useless. Although he lost the use of his hands, he gained prestige for showing that not only did he have servants to tend to his every need, but he also had the enormous rice balls to grow fingernails through his own hands.

Usually, a disabled person can be defined as someone who lacks the ability to achieve the things his culture deems important, but an easier way to tell might be to take note of who the kids in the neighborhood like to throw rocks at. Occasionally the label "handicapped" is created through prejudice. Some perceive race, age, or sex as a handicap. Often, once labeled, a person will begin to behave according to this stereotype. Even the most robust elderly person can feel old when confronted with such folksy colloquialisms as "long in the tooth," "over the hill," or "a decaying, diaper-wearing fossil."

Some troubled crafters can be identified at birth, others slip happily along through life, openly accepted by all those blind to the mayhem lurking beneath. It is not until faced with the prospect of shaping a lump of clay into something other than a lump of clay, that the mental, physical, or emotional bedlam is revealed. The truth is, the streets are cluttered with these shambling misfits who go unnoticed and are casually dismissed as normal crafters.

So how do we define the handicapped crafter? Simply, a handicapped crafter is challenged on some level by things a normal crafter might take for granted. In other words, they have hurdles to overcome in order to achieve their creative goal.

What are these hurdles? They range from obsessive-compulsive disorder to drug addiction, from stress-induced paralysis to clinical laziness. Any affliction, condition, or predilection that can make it more difficult to whittle a stick into a pointer or turn a soup can into a pencil holder is considered a hurdle.

But why then expend the energy attempting to craft with barriers in your path? The reason is this: every human is faced with some hurdle in life they must fight to overcome, and the only way to overcome that hurdle is to continue to challenge it. Handicapped crafters need to get into the craft room and challenge their disabilities, whether it be restless leg syndrome, canine hip dysplasia, or lengthy beard. The good news is that not only is it positive to challenge yourself, but the act of crafting is actually healing in and of itself.

The Healing Power of Crafting

Terminal cancer patients have been encouraged to paint pictures focused on shrinking their tumor; in the same way, while crafting, one can imagine sticking googly eyes on a cancerous growth so that it seems friendly and lovable. Some scientists say repetitive crafts, such as all of them, can actually induce a relaxation response. The act of doing a task over and over again breaks the monotonous train of everyday thoughts, such as boredom from doing the same thing over and over again.

The best argument, though, for encouraging handicapped crafters to get in the workroom is that at least then they are participating. Just because a crafter is bedridden, delusional, or feels compelled to wear their pants hanging around their knees in an attempt to make a fashion statement is no reason that they can't feel useful.

This chapter about crafting disabilities differs from most other craft books on this subject in that the authors of this book have no medical, clinical, or any other type of expertise in this area. The authors have merely followed a line of hearsay and filled in the holes with random conjecture. The following crafts in this section were chosen specifically with hurdles in mind, and are simple enough not to belittle handicapped crafters. Hopefully, the finished products will look complex enough to create the illusion that some skill was involved.

Many of these projects were tried out on all sorts of handicapped crafters, ranging from the physically abled but mentally chaotic to the mentally capable and physically uproarious. The results, for the most part, had to be either discarded or burned but the efforts made were encouraging.

JEAN'S CORNER

Do you know what I learned? Keeping my old paws busy with crafting is a cure-all for most things. I used to have an anger management problem, or at least those are the fancy words a very unpleasant judge gave to my habit of attacking my husband Gene when the urge struck. I am not claiming that I never crossed a line, because I didn't know a line existed until a court of law told me so. But now, when Gene does something that annoys me, like walking into a room that I'm in, or talking to me, and I feel my blood beginning to percolate, I'll just go in my craft room and knit, or bead, or go behind the house and hammer on the hood of Gene's truck. The point is, I'm turning my rage into something creative, and that creativity has a relaxing effect.

The following section discusses some of the more common obstacles facing potential crafters. It also supplies a list of craft suggestions that were chosen specifically for each hurdle they address. Hopefully these will act as a starting point on what will prove to be a bumpy road, fraught with pitfalls, potholes, and hairpin turns, and littered with the felt, yarn, and pompon fragments of the many crafts gone bad. Good luck!

ADD

Crafting involves paying close attention to details, following instructions, being well organized, and finishing a task, while ADD involves the inability to focus long enough to make it through this sentence. Crafts that are perfect for those with ADD fall into two categories: A. Those that have no beginning or end and can be worked on whenever the motivation strikes, and B. Crafts that are connected to a crisis situation where focus is essential to maintain life, such as defusing a bomb. This book will focus on category A.

Crafting with ADD!
RADIATOR POLE WRAP

Instructions: Radiator pipes can get very hot when the heat is on, not to mention they often look drab. Jazz up your pipe and make it safer by wrapping rope around the pole while your mind wanders. Note: Also makes an ideal scratching post for those cats who are fortunate enough to still have claws.

Chronic Pain

Here is a quick test: if you were suffering from acute agonizing pain, would you rather ingest a narcotic and sail away on the warm mellow waves of numbness, or craft something out of torn pieces of crepe paper? So far 100% of those polled have picked drugs, but because this is a craft book, we skewed those poll numbers to suggest crepe paper crafts! Sewing tiny stitches, beadwork, cutting crepe paper, and other intricate projects are all appropriate for crafters with chronic pain, because these types of crafts force the chronic pain folks to focus on something other than their pain.

Crafting While in Chronic Pain!
BEADED PHOTO ALBUM

Instructions: Using tweezers to hold them, glue tiny beads on a Popsicle stick photo album you made when you were in less pain.

Autism

The autistic are often perfectionists, which makes crafting an unnatural fit for them, because most of the projects randomly slapped together by the average crafter can barely be identified as a craft. Seldom does the word "perfect" come to mind while viewing a "toilet paper roll duck bank."

Crafting and Autistic!
KIT POTHOLDERS

Perfectionists enjoy having a clear understanding of what the finished project is supposed to look like. Models, kits, and puzzles are excellent crafts for these types of crafters, because the picture is right on the box.

Hard of Hearing

Being hard of hearing is not a significant deterrent to crafting. In most cases it is a benefit. Anybody who has been part of a crafting circle and forced to listen to "Marjorie" talking about the "funny" things her cat "Tiddlepus" does will know what I'm talking about. One drawback for the hard of hearing in terms of crafting can be collecting materials, especially from the natural world. How many more hard-of-hearing crafters have to be maimed while in the forest collecting nuts during hunting season, or run down in the street looking for bottle caps, before some regulations are enacted?

Crafting While Hard of Hearing!
COTTON BALL RAIN CLOUD (SEE PAGE 285)

Instructions: Cut out the shape of a cloud from gray construction paper. Apply cotton balls. Paint gray. To apply the "drops," dangle strings from the clouds. Tape teardrop-shaped gray construction paper to the ends of the strings.

Anger

Crafting while angry can be very dangerous; for instance, when throwing pots, the angry tend to actually throw pots. (See Mosaics.) This can lead to multiple head injuries for your crafting circle. The key for the angry crafter is to find a project where the anger can be directed toward the creative process and not the skulls of co-crafters.

Crafting While Angry!

DISTRESSING A BOX

Instructions: Drag a pair of scissors across the box, randomly stabbing it like you would a lover who has spurned you. Using a lit match, burn the corners. Complete the box by whipping it with a chain.

Warning: Do not craft on a carpet, indoors, or within eye or earshot of the authorities.

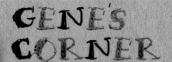

GENE'S CORNER

I can be a pretty angry guy, but unlike Jean, I don't need to hit things in order to make the rage subside. Although, guess what? I'm thinking about having my lawyer hit her, hit her up, that is, with a subpoena because of her last episode. Anyway, I've found a much more peaceful way to vent my fury and it's through the beautiful and melodic words of my poetry. I hate to say it, but I'm a natural, hell, that last sentence alone is almost poetry and I wasn't even trying. The point is, I've found a positive way to express myself and nobody's car hood has to be dented. Look, I'm not saying I never feel like taking a poke at my wife. I'm not saying I don't fantasize about her demise. But guess what? Now when I feel like putting my fingers around her neck, I put them around a pencil instead and I just let the feelings flow all over the goddamn page.

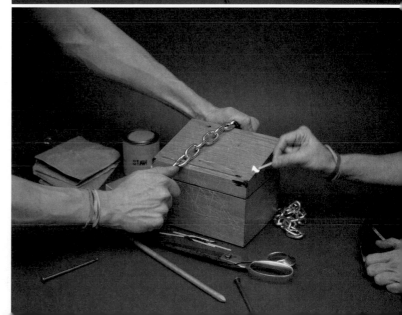

Sandbags

*Your depression is sandbags for the
   happy to carry
Sad sacks filled up with despair
   and misery
Sinking good times like a boat that
   is shoddy
Like rocks in a bag to load down
   the body
A heavy heart keeps the party
   well-moored
Making sure the fun stays floored
Your melancholic millstone causes
   a strain
Psychological tonnage, forever a drain
So on your next invite, here's a
   revelation
Stay home, don't show, or get
   medication.*

            —Gene Woodchuck

Depression

Your Depression Is Our Sandbag

If you are a depressed person, here are some things you've come to learn: employers don't want to hire you knowing you will be unable to contribute to the bawdy watercooler gossip like normal workers do. You are almost always moved to the bottom of the party guest list, for fear that your condition might bum out the other party guests. No one asks you to watch their dog, knowing that after spending a few days with you, Buster always returns with suicidal tendencies. But here is something that you depressed people are probably not aware of—did you know you are a burden to friends and family? This one is often overlooked, because friends and family are usually too polite to bring it up, but you should hear the awful things they are saying about you behind your back.

One night, while having difficulty getting through a weaving exercise, my crafting coach pointed out to me I was carrying all my "mental baggage" into the craft room. He told me, "Your worries and concerns are like sandbags that weigh you down." To illustrate his point, he filled up bags with sand and had me hold them while attempting to weave a floral Navajo afghan. The results, I can tell you, were neither Navajo nor Afghan. Lesson learned! In the same way, your depression is like sandbags that normal people have to carry, weighing them down, and not allowing them to kick up their heels. How can someone with depression avoid this uncomfortable situation? Awareness. In order to remind those of you who you already know who I am talking about—what you are doing to others—crafting miniature sandbags is the perfect craft for you.

Instructions: Fill tiny muslin sacks with sand, kitty litter, or dried beans. Cinch with dung-colored twine.

Elderly

The most difficult part of being elderly is being old. By old, of course, we mean grizzledly dodderyingly well past one's prime. Just because a person has one foot in the grave, doesn't mean the other tootsie can't be lightly planted in the craft room. The key is to find crafts that don't take a lot of energy, can be completed in spurts, and for which the completion point is quick to get to, or even better, can be left vague. Here is a lively idea for the almost dead.

Crafting While Elderly!
GRANNY'S PILLOWCASES

Instructions: Use markers to fill in a pattern on a case instead of using a sharp needle and tangly thread. Find a comfortable position in bed. Fill in pattern in between naps. Fun!

GRAY

LEMON

BLUE

PINK

RED

LIME

ROSE

HOT PINK

GREEN

SILVER

TEAL

GOLD

BURGUNDY

ORANGE

TAN

SLATE

VIOLET

BLACK

Mood Chart

Bipolar Disorder

People with bipolar disorder suffer from fluctuations in their brain chemistry that cause an extreme ebb and flow of the emotional state, much like a beach that has its lowest and highest tide in the same day, or like the McDLT, which was uniquely packaged to keep "the hot side hot and the cold side cold." Bipolar people need a craft that can simultaneously engage their manic side, keeping them focused on the task at hand, while also suiting their depressed side. Because bipolar disorder is a cyclical disease, the craft must serve this merry-go-round of chaos. The Rusty Nail Wind Chime is the perfect project for these types of disabled crafters.

Crafting While Bipolar!

RUSTY NAIL WIND CHIME

Instructions: On an emotional downswing, toss a fistful of nails into your backyard. At a later date, during a manic phase, search the yard for what are now rusty nails. Once collected, string them together to make a wind chime.

Poor Eyesight

Good eyesight is not essential for crafting. Even the projects of crafters not inhibited with weak eyes are often described by those who view them as "fuzzy-shaped doodads," or "amorphous shadowy something on my mantel." Whether you can see or not doesn't seem to make much difference in the world of crafting, especially where the finished product is concerned. Still, it does seem helpful to work with materials that are tactile. Pinecones, hobnob glass, clay, and pipe cleaners are all good materials for the poor of eyesight.

Crafting with Poor Eyesight!
DECORATED PINECONES (SEE PAGE 54)
Instructions: Self-explanatory.

Clay Duck

Fashionably Long Fingernails

On the list of most difficult hurdles one might try to overcome to become a successful crafter, fashionably long fingernails is near the top. There is no other activity you can engage in, including surgery and puppetry, in which hands are more essential than crafting. Fashionably long fingernails make it virtually impossible to get close to the materials you will need to complete your project. Luckily, there are ways to work around this horrible yet fashionable affliction.

1 Learn to operate your nails like chopsticks.
2 Imagine your nails to be tiny putty knives.
3 Watch nature films to discover how raptors use their talons.

You will find that fashionably long nails are actually an asset in some situations, such as playing guitar, or digging stencils out of a compartment box. Here are a couple craft ideas for you to try.

Crafting with Fashionably Long Fingernails!
ROCK CANDY (SEE ABOVE AND PAGE 158)

POTATO SHIPS
Instructions: Bake a potato. Stick wooden skewers though a slice of cheese to make a sail. You will find your nails are perfect for placing mushroom caps on the top. Set sail!

Potato Ships

Multiple Personality Disorder

Most experts on the subject would say that multiple personality disorder is a complex struggle within one person in which two or more distinct identities grapple for control. I say, based on the extensive research I've done watching *The Three Faces of Eve*, and that other one starring the Flying Nun, it is just another example of the human brain making a silk purse from lemons. Yes, this severe form of dissociation is born from extreme and violent trauma during early childhood, but the upside is, in its attempt to detach itself from this hellish nightmare, the brain creates an immensely entertaining, cinemaworthy circus of personalities. It's as if a playwright has stuffed a lengthy scenario into your skull and you get to play all the characters, but you don't have to remember any lines or even when to enter or exit! Spending time with a person who has multiple personality disorder is a revolving door of amusement. Sometimes the personality is shy and demure and then for no reason at all, it turns sexy! Then before you can adjust to this saucy vamp, an innocent child emerges. What a thrilling roller-coaster ride. I would love to rent one of these delightful lunatics to liven up my next office party!

I do find one thing upsetting about multiple personality disorder. Each personality seems so different from the other one, yet they all kind of dress the same. Perhaps the top button is opened, or a scarf is adjusted, but there is not a whole lot of change. To address this problem that most of our "experts" seem to be more than willing to ignore, I've included ideas throughout this book for crafting simple costumes that are worthy of even the most radical personality change.

Crafting with Multiple Personalities!
COSTUME MAKING (SEE PAGES 294–295)

Obsessive-Compulsive Disorder

People with OCD often make superb crafters. They have a preoccupation with details, lists, order, and organization, and they tend to be hoarders. Hoarders are good for crafting on both sides of the coin. They are a good source of crafting materials, such as scraps of cloth, pieces of wood, buttons, and springs, and on the other side, other than Mom, they are about the only people who won't toss your craft away as soon as they peel out of your driveway. So why are they included in the section on hurdles? The answer is inflexibility. Crafting is a fluid art form. Often what starts out as a nutcracker finger puppet ends up as a patchwork gypsy shawl. This can be maddening to the obsessive-compulsive crafter. The best crafts for these people are simple crafts that are only ever going to be what they are.

Crafting While Obsessive-Compulsive!
UNCANNY CAN CHARACTERS

Ever notice those old, flattened rusty cans by the side of the road? Those sure are an eyesore. Maybe you'll pick that one up because it's the eco-friendly thing to do. Okay, there is another one. Might as well get that one, too. Perhaps you'll walk down the road a bit because the thought of another can lying on the side of the road just doesn't seem right … Guess what? Now you can turn your garbage-collecting obsession into offbeat art. Scrub clean the flattened cans you have collected and paint amusing characters on them. See how many you can collect!

Wheelchair-Bound

Just because a person is confined to a wheelchair is no reason they should not participate. Yes, it can be an effort to add the wheelchair-bound to a crafting circle. It will mean ramps, grab bars, speed rails, and special tables that are chair height, not to mention the horrible guilt you will have when during an emergency evacuation you leave "ole wheelie" behind under the panicky unstated "every man for himself" policy. But being wheelchair-bound is not a great hindrance to crafting, so here are a couple craft ideas that might be fun to do as well as useful to the wheelchair-bound.

Crafting While Wheelchair-Bound!
HEEL-LESS SOCKS

Heel-less socks are sensible for wheelchair-bound folks because they don't have to worry about their heel matching up with the sock heel. Knit socks in tube form.

FINGERLESS GLOVES

Instructions: Knit fingerless gloves. If this seems confusing, knit gloves and snip the fingers off.

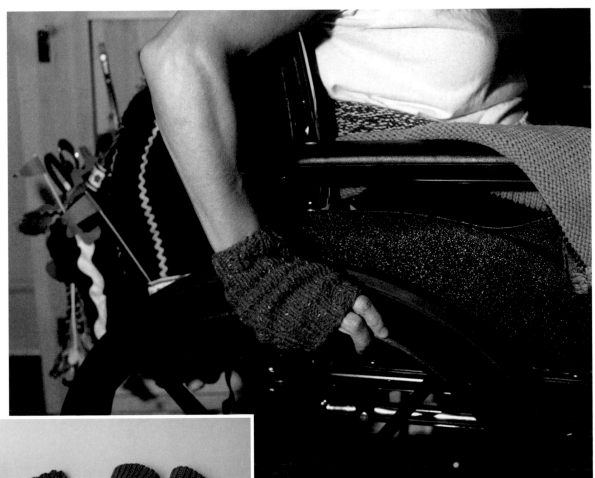

Jean's Tips for the Wheelchair-Bound

Buttons and zippers are better going down the front and side than the back. Slacks can be made for the sitting position instead of the standing position.

CUI: CRAFTING UNDER THE INFLUENCE

Boozing

Crafting While Boozing!

BOTTLE CAP CASTANETS

Instructions: Punch holes in the tops of 2 bottle caps. Fish both ends of a pipe cleaner through the holes, leaving a loop. Twist pipe cleaner on the underside to secure. Put on fingertips and make noise clanging them together.

Beer Bottle Cap Castanets

You can cast your vote or plaster cast
Be cast adrift in the ocean vast
Cast your eyes upon those you've just met
As for me I'll just castanet.

Made from bottle caps I click in time
I play with the music, don't cost me a dime.
Caps from beer drunk with little regret
I love my bottle cap castanets.

When I feel the urge to dance and clack
Off to the liquor store, for a musical
twelve-pack
My ex-wife and former boss can continue to fret
Can't hear what they're saying, only my
castanets.
—Gene Woodchuck

CHAMPAGNE CORKS!

Ramped Up on Amphetamines

The pills accelerate the brain, thinking so quick, on the fly, ideas flow faster and faster, faster than the ability to communicate, faster than the ability to keep up with your hands, so awake, ahead of the last thoughts, thinking things that haven't even come to the brain, thinking out there before it's even in here, what was I thinking before I was thinking, heart is cranking, thump thump thump.

Crafting While Ramped Up on Amphetamines!

List of Crafts: All of them.

Instructions: I feel good, you feel good, good, feel like crafting, just start doing them, all of them, one at a time or two at once or whatever, know what I'm saying, know what I'm saying, you know, you know, you know, taping and gluing and cutting, wow, they're coming together, it's all taking shape, all of it and everything, snip snip, staple staple, glue and glue, wait how 'bout making one giant craft out of all them, all the crafts together, every one into a supercraft!

Tripping on Hallucinogens

Hallucinogens are strong mood-changing drugs with unpredictable psychological effects. For crafters facing this hurdle, it is best to pick crafts for which, when finished, looking warped and contorted is a virtue. An ideal craft would be "a curved and misshaped kaleidoscope flowing through mother-of-pearl spigots that morph into timeless wolf heads of wood-grained color," but also high on the list, the Distorted Spiderweb.

DISTORTED SPIDERWEB

Instructions: With a needle and embroidery twine, begin to thread a random pattern using the inside of a box as a loom. Weave from one side of the box to the borderless astral plane, taking care to encompass all reality, and then let go, realizing that the boundaries are an illusion and the inner voice speaks, in shadows and paint, of a cellophane all-powerful presence, and the ethereal shapes are bent as time buckles in sparkles and splash until the ego melts and is gone!

TRIPPY

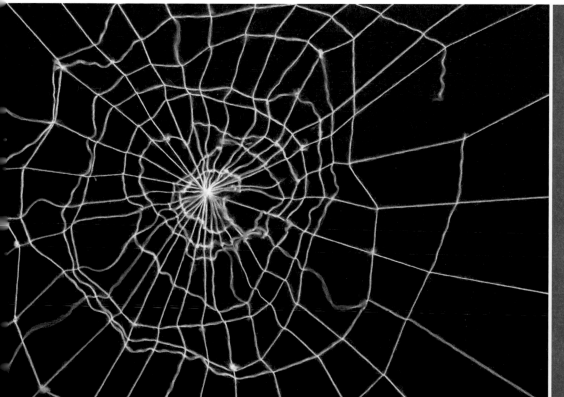

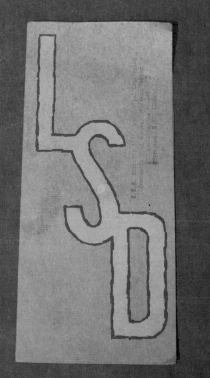

Marihuana
(The Weed of Madness)

Pot addicts are likely to encounter the following two difficulties while crafting: 1. They won't start a project, and, 2. They won't finish a project. That's because marihuana is a liar. This "herby" propagandist convinces those who "par-toke" that "hanging out" is "cool." Well it's not cool! You know what else is not cool? The warm euphoria, the openness, and the easy flow of ideas that are the sinister realities this roadside weed deals in. For the reefer fiend, fancy becomes folly, tedious becomes thrilling, and the horrible becomes hilarious. Just imagine a dark world where people are in a perpetual state of peace and amusement. It can be a difficult decision, considering whether to allow these grass ghouls into your craft circle. The thought of mixing with Mexicans and jazz musicians is always unsettling. But like all handicapped crafters, they deserve at least some initial support on a healthy crafter's part.

Crafting While Under the Weed of Madness

CHIANTI CANDLE

Instructions: A Chianti candle is a good craft for the jolly green junkie, because it is never really finished.

Empty a Chianti bottle (in the sink!), and insert dripping candle into the spout of the bottle. Place in front of an open window so the breeze will make the flame flicker, causing the wax to run down the sides of the bottle.

Adding a Handicapped Crafter to Your Crafting Circle

If you are a person who will be assisting a crippled crafter, or rather, a handicraftable crafter, be aware that most people have no desire to spend time with these types of crafters, for they can be depressing and exhausting. This person requires patience. So keep projects simple and brief in duration to compensate for short attention spans and emotional frustration, and have emergency numbers posted and plenty of sweets on hand. When working with the handicraftable, you will encounter a wide range of behaviors: for example, with a little help and guidance, one disabled crafter might be able to mold a simple ashtray, while another troubled crafter might set all the felt ablaze while screaming for more fudge (see page 142). Another might be cooperative, undemanding, and a pleasure to craft with, while still another might go off like a battery in a microwave. Some will nap most of the afternoon. Yet others will babble incoherently while taking a hostage and can only be talked down with the promise of cheese.

Whenever dealing with disabled crafters, you must be careful and focused, but the truth is, no single precaution can protect you from every crafter that we call disabled. The best that can be hoped for is that once in your care, these somewhat erratic and occasionally drooly misfits will stay focused on the task before them while avoiding permanent incarceration. They must be allowed to craft at their own speed, but most importantly, they must be treated exactly the same way one would treat a normal crafter, if that normal crafter were radically unpredictable and sporadically threatening.

JEAN'S CORNER

Beads are difficult to keep track of even if you are an unafflicted crafter. Beads! What I do is use those jumbo seven-day pill organizers to hold all my beads so they won't get away from me! I find cupcake tins work for this purpose as well.

Being blind can be quite a burden. I don't see so well in the dark, so something I do is place multiple bottles of milk of magnesia in the bathroom cabinet. That way, at night, if I'm looking for a night crème, say something avocado-based, and I accidently grab the milk of magnesia and mistakenly apply it to my face, guess what, so what. It turns out milk of magnesia makes a terrific face mask. Crisis averted.

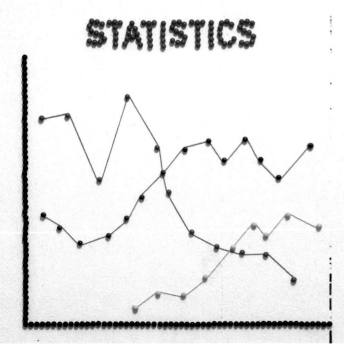

STATISTICS

Thumbtacks!

Popsicle Sticks!

113

Safety Meeting

Wink, blink, wink, blink
Remember, always, everybody think!
Splinter in the eye, the white has turned to pink
Infection caused some swelling, should have
rinsed it in the sink.
Eyelid swollen shut in a permanent wink
Didn't follow precautions posted in black ink.
—Gene Woodchuck

By this point in the book, you're knee-deep in elbow macaroni. Congratulations, and yes, that *is* a lovely pasta collage. You have now discovered the joy of crafting, but you have also learned that with crafting comes slicing, sticking, slitting, and slashing. A multitude of perils looms over the craft room, not to mention the additional menace that is snakes. Crafting mishaps range from paper cuts to murder. We will discuss the array of hazards lying in wait, and some precautions you can take.

"You're Going to Lose an Eye"

Consider this statistic: 86 percent of all craft room accidents are the fault of the person involved, and of these, 96 percent are blamed on either the person next to that person or a spiteful God. Reckless crafting causes eight times the number of accidents caused by faulty glue guns and snakes combined! Equipment training can significantly reduce craft room accidents, but unfortunately it can also increase craft room homicides due to IPR (Implement Proficiency Resentment). But statistics suggest that it is more likely for a crafter to be badly scorched because of incompetence using a wood-burning tool than to be bludgeoned to death by a jealous fellow crafter because of one's mastery of said implement.

Crafting: A Party of One

The best protection from crafting injuries is to avoid other crafters. This is not a general dismissal of crafting clubs or a negative judgment about those who choose to craft in pairs, including same-sex crafting or even multiple-partner crafting known as "decoupage à trois." This just means that when crafting with others, take sensible precautions. Don't share buttons. Divvy up felt scraps before crafting. Never go dutch on the dry flowers.

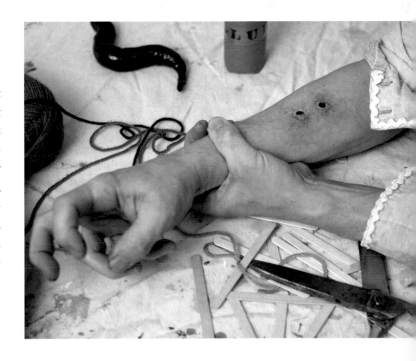

Know Your Tool

Not only do you need the right tool for the right job, you need the right knowledge for the right tool for the right job, otherwise known as the "golden triangle" or the "right triangle," not to be confused with a "right triangle." A "right triangle" has one angle that is 90 degrees. The "right triangle" has three points representing the elements you will need to get the job done efficiently without mangling a finger or worse. Even with the proper command of the right tool, maiming can still be part of the equation. Take an axe for instance. Statistics show us that when the swinging of a heavy axe is combined with the close proximity of appendages, regardless of mastery, occasionally, something dear will be inadvertently chopped free from your torso. In this situation, always be mindful to leave a smooth, clean stump.

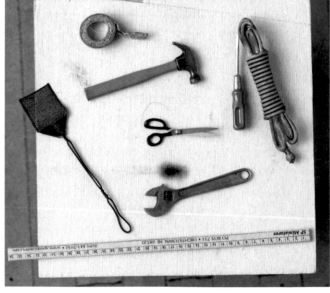

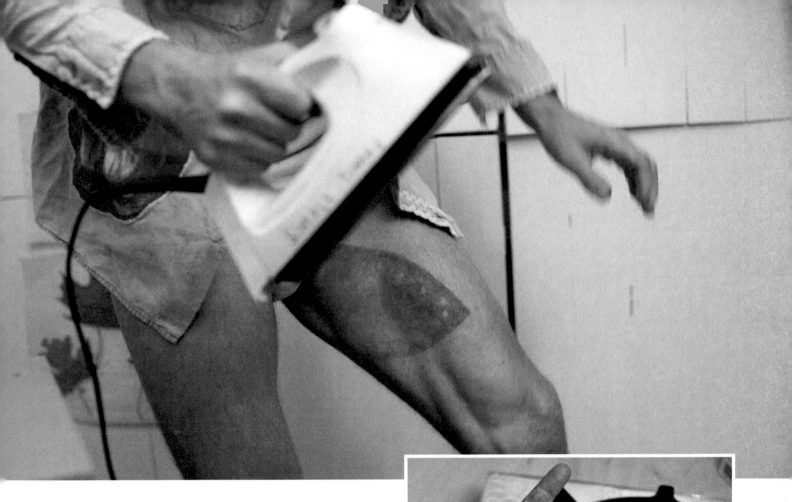

Shortcuts Lead to Long Cuts

Crafters often make rash decisions that they hope will make the job faster. But often, these time-savers make the job more risky. Take pressing leaves between two pieces of wax paper, for instance. Ironing one at a time seems sensible. It's easy to focus and make sure each one is done right. But what if five wax paper leaves were laid in a row? That would mean five done in the time it would usually take to do one?! What could possibly go wrong?

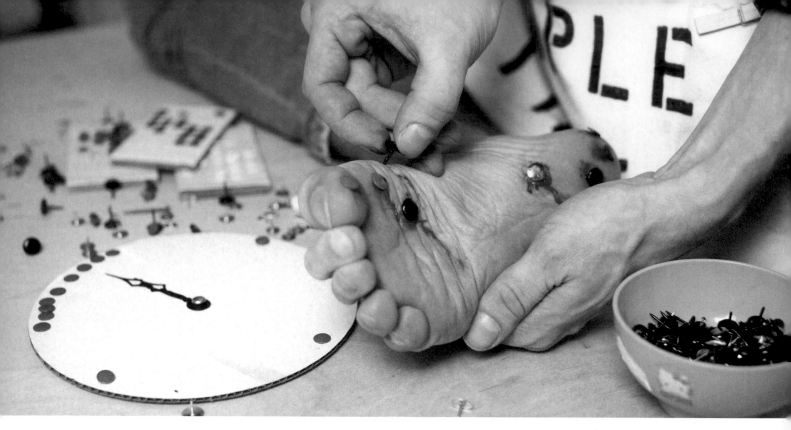

Messy Workspace

It is important to keep your work area well organized. A disorderly craft room creates all sorts of dangers, from tripping hazards, to nesting opportunities for snakes. In feng shui tradition, it is believed that a vital force, or chi, should be able to flow unobstructed around the space of the workroom, but after you've impaled a hand with a misplaced knitting needle a stagnated chi will be the least of your concerns.

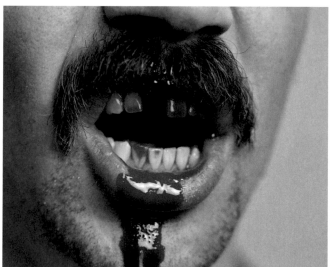

Overconfidence

Confidence can be a wonderful thing. Overconfidence can be a dangerous thing, often leading to hilariously tragic results. Whenever a crafter announces, "Hey, I have a better way to do that," the result is sure to be a violent, albeit rib-tickling, one.

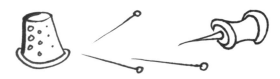

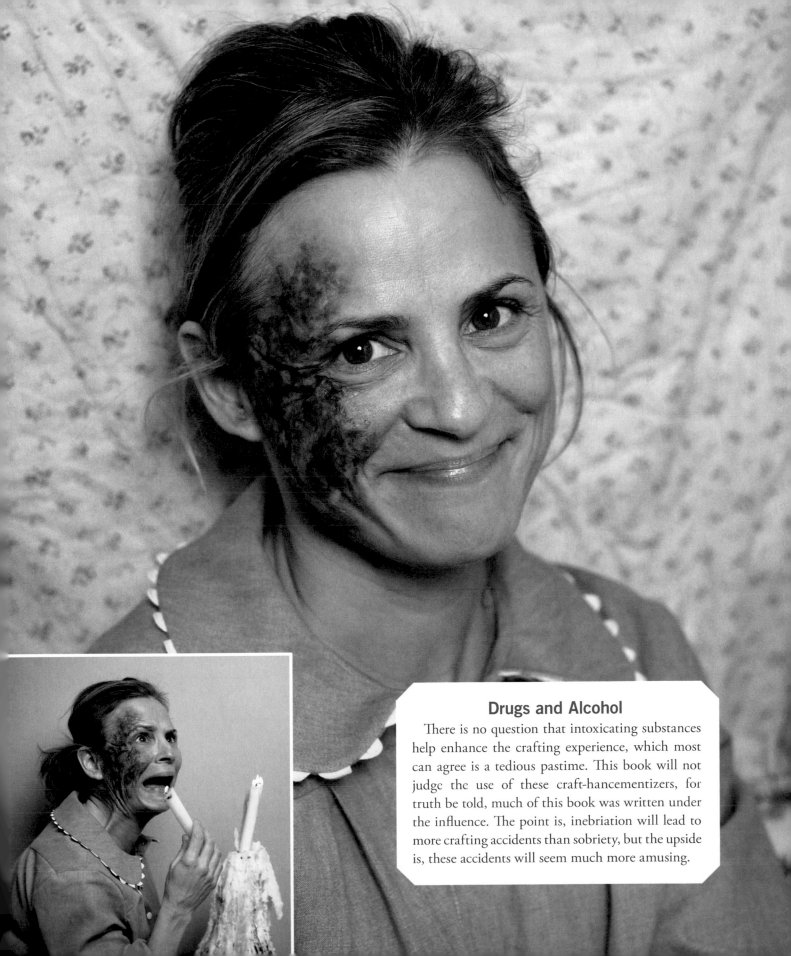

Drugs and Alcohol

There is no question that intoxicating substances help enhance the crafting experience, which most can agree is a tedious pastime. This book will not judge the use of these craft-hancementizers, for truth be told, much of this book was written under the influence. The point is, inebriation will lead to more crafting accidents than sobriety, but the upside is, these accidents will seem much more amusing.

Craft Place Homicides

After a spike a few years ago, there has been a slight fall, continuing a mild declining trend in craft place homicides. This is no reason to be complacent. Although the downturn is positive, the craft room still ranks second only to nursing homes in workplace-related homicides. There are some obvious safety measures you can take. Never craft with strangers. Picking up hitchhikers and beading can be a lethal combination. Avoid tatting with anyone who describes himself as either "an out-of-work handyman" or "a bit of a loner." Any middle-aged man who still sleeps with his mother, in spite of his fondness for "pinch potting," would be a bad risk. But often the most serious threat comes from the people you know best and suspect least. It only takes one minor incident to trigger "raku rage," or "embroider envy." Steering clear of overcelebrating your crafting triumphs can greatly reduce the risk of a member of your crafting circle turning on you with catastrophic results.

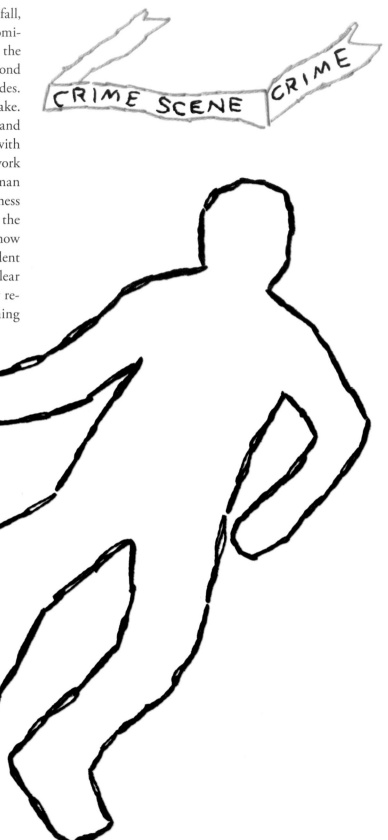

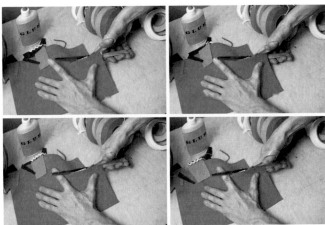

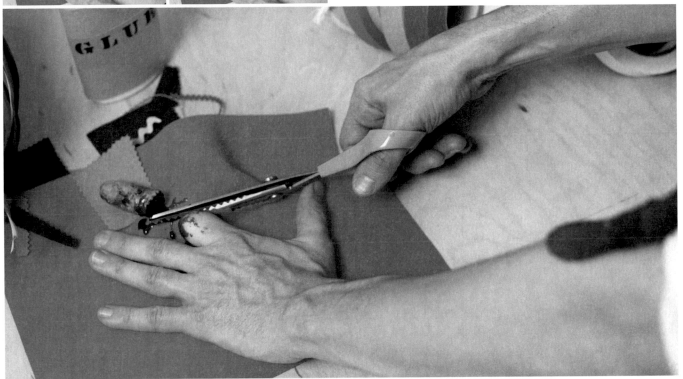

Safety Meeting

Crafting will be an enjoyable and fulfilling activity as long as you take precautions to assure safety, and you accept that you, as well as many of the crafters nearest and dearest to you, are statistically destined to be hurt real bad.

Stretching Before Crafting

It is crucial to keep yourself limber before crafting. The better the range of motion of your muscles, the better they can handle the rigors of crafting. Nothing causes lumbar tension quite like the act of dribble waxing. When crafting, every part of the body is tested, which is why it's important to stretch from head to toe. That means rotating joints, extending the trunk, grinding the gluteus, maximizing the maximus. Flex anything that dangles. Contract all that wobbles. Leave no tendon unturned. If you are part of a crafting circle it is helpful to stretch in pairs. Don't put a lot of thought into it, just grab for the first thing on your partner you can get a hold of and tug. In many cases though, most crafters will be elasticizing solo. Here is a helpful guide you can follow.

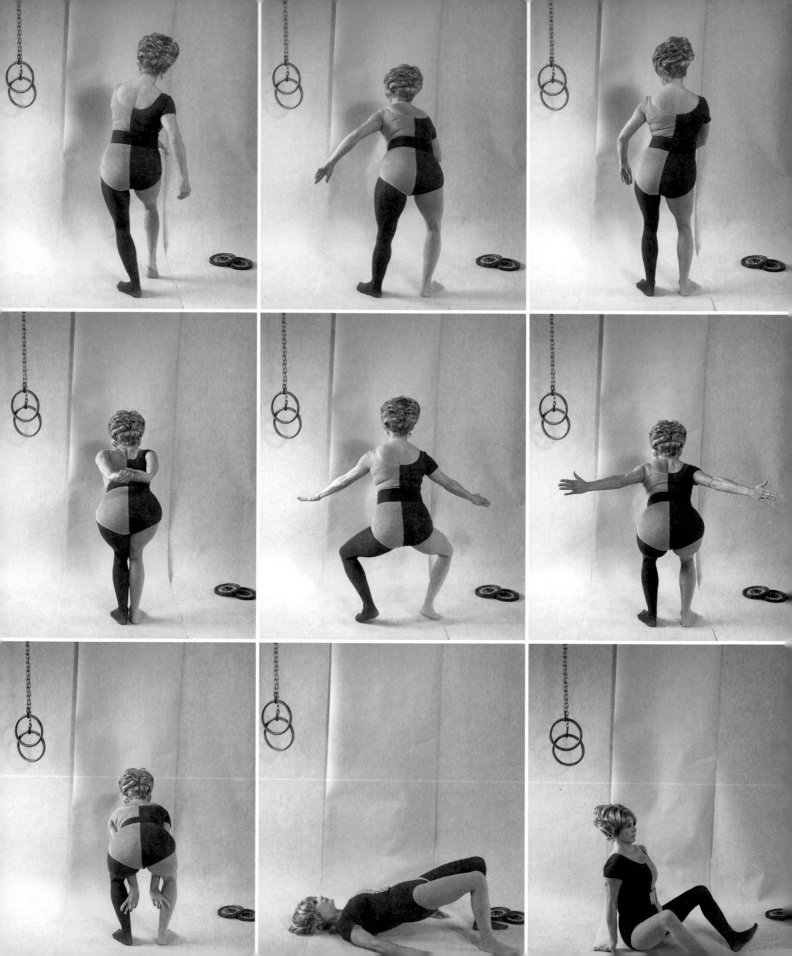

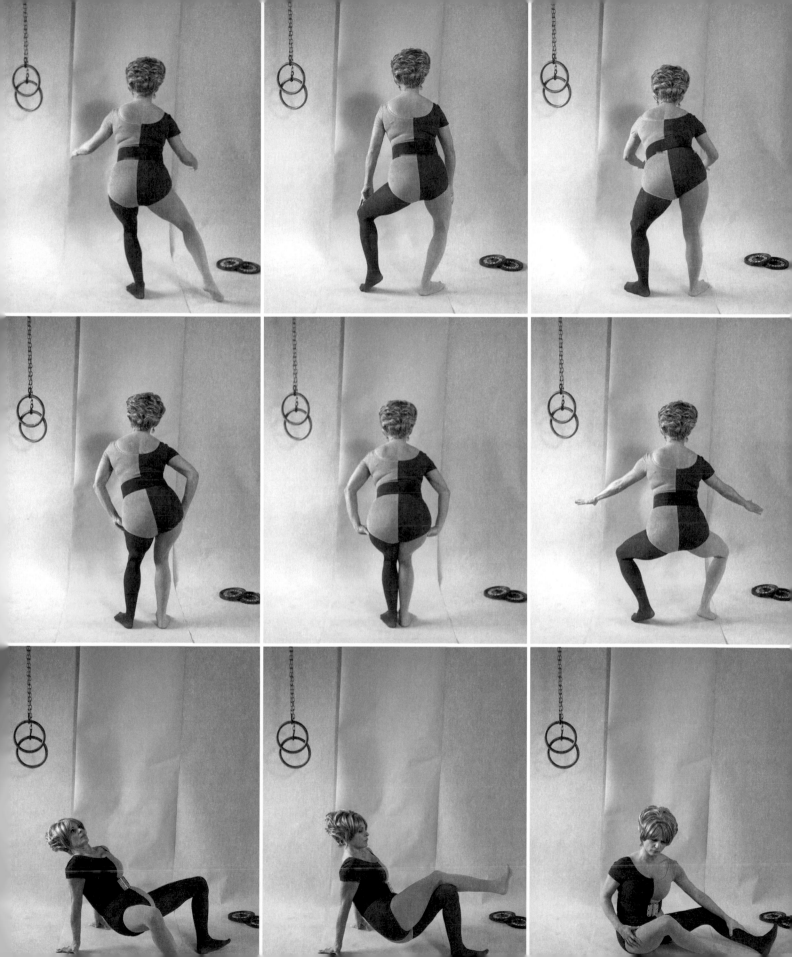

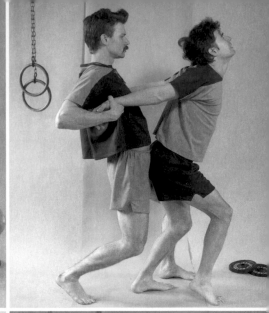

Stretching After Crafting

Even for those crafters who are careful to prepare for the workroom, the strains of crafting can take their toll. Very few crafters, including the most hearty, can forever withstand the severity of hooking in a hurry, the vigorous glue bottle shake, or repetitive ribboning. After a demanding afternoon of project making, you will find ligaments swollen and muscle fibers tender, and it's important to work these out before they spread to the more vulnerable parts of your body, such as the kidneys, the nerve center, and the genitals. Stretching with partners is the most effective way to work out what is troubling you because it increases the torque factor, and when you are experiencing scapula soreness due to stitching, or acute tatting tenderness, you are going to want maximum torque.

AT REST

Crafting for the dead serves many purposes. It memorializes the deceased, it comforts the grievers, and it presents the opportunity to hit the craft room. Sure, it might seem appropriate to show up at a funeral with a lovely bouquet of real lilies in hand, but for only a few cents and about the time it takes to crumble a wad of paper, you can craft artificial-flower-like bogus blooms out of crepe paper!

When a friend or acquaintance dies, your first reaction may be to physically or emotionally comfort the bereaved, but mine is to craft. Some would say the best gift you could give to someone mourning is a roasted chicken. Let's try something. Replace the words "roasted chicken," with the words "pompon wiggle worm" and then read it again. Although the sentence is no longer accurate, doesn't it feel better?

It is always awkward attempting to find words to comfort a griever. There are the somewhat soothing but obvious clichés: "I'm sorry for your loss"; "I always thought you'd go first"; "I hope you're not blaming yourself—if it was your fault, you'd probably be in jail right now"; or "I don't mean to second guess, but, do you think an open casket was the appropriate way to go?" I believe everything that needs to be said to anyone who has just lost a loved one can be easily summed up with some sequins, a fistful of Popsicle sticks, and household glue.

Losing a Pet

Sometimes losing a pet is more painful then losing a human because in the case of the pet, you were not pretending to love it. We are responsible for the well-being of our pets, so it is hard not to feel some sort of guilt when they pass. But too often our heads are filled with unproductive nagging questions, causing us to second-guess and blame ourselves for something that was clearly the pet's fault: "If only I hadn't left him tied to that grocery cart while shopping for chicken thighs and lighter fluid"; "I thought the bag was the tank"; "I figured it would save time if I declawed it myself"; "If only I had cleaned the cage the traditional way instead of employing the magnificent suctioning power of a Shop-Vac." Having guilt about the loss of a pet only takes away from that giddy feeling of replacing it with a younger, fluffier one. When pet owners feel guilty, they clearly are not taking into account the all too common, but little spoken about, phenomenon of pet suicide.

Often the people around you will not understand the grief you feel about the loss of your pet. They will say

things like: "What's the big deal, it was only an animal," or "Hell, if you cared so much, why did you leave it tied to a grocery cart?" The first assumption here is that pets are somehow less important than people. The truth is pets can be more important to our health and well-being than any of the humans around us. They provide constant companionship and unwavering loyalty and they never ask to borrow money.

Crafting for our fallen pets is a wonderful healer. First of all, it gives us something to focus on other than our grief, and more importantly, it affords us a means to memorialize "Mr. Twinkles," "Puddles McFluffybum," or "Queen Fussyfuzz" with the dignity they deserve.

JEAN'S CORNER

I had Great Danes for years. It's a big dog to bury, especially if you have a small backyard. If you cremate something this big you need to make sure you get all the ashes, they always try to shortchange you. The same goes for humans, they never give you all the remains unless you ask for them.

Sentimental Jewelry

Often serial killers will take trophies of their victims: an item of clothing, a finger, the entire skin, and even some items that most would consider gruesome. If you take away the unfortunate fact that serial killers hunt, capture, torture, and murder innocent victims, there is something slightly charming about maniacs wanting to memorialize their conquests. In the same way, crafting can be used to preserve the memory of a loved one, be it a pet or a relative. With a little creative zeal, a lock of hair can be transformed into a wearable monument, and nobody is going to shut you away for that.

CROSS

MATERIALS – CERAMIC-LIKE SCULPTING COMPOUND
ROLLING PIN   OVEN   2" PAINT BRUSH
KNIFE   BAKING SHEET   FLAT WHITE PAINT
- ROLL OUT SCULPTING COMPOUND 1/4 INCH THICK WITH ROLLING PIN
- USING A KNIFE CUT OUT A CROSS SHAPE
- BAKE IN THE OVEN (FOLLOW DIRECTIONS ON BOX)
- LET COOL
- TO FORM BASE MAKE SMALL BALL OF SCULPTING COMPOUND AND PUSH BOTTOM OF THE CROSS INTO IT. REMOVE CROSS AND BAKE THE BASE IN THE OVEN. (FOLLOW DIRECTIONS ON BOX) LET COOL.
- PAINT CROSS AND BASE WITH TEN COATS OF FLAT WHITE PAINT.

R.I.P.

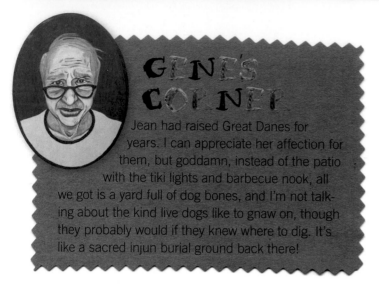

MOUSE MATCH-TRESS DEATHBED

When you sense that your mouse has reached the final spin on his wheel, you can create a deathbed that will transition nicely into a final resting place out of a few simple supplies.

Materials:

A small box of matches

Some of that quilted paper from inside a box of chocolates

A paper napkin

Glue

Scissors

Instructions: Empty the matches out of a new box of large oven matches, or use an old box whose matches have already been used. Save a few matches for the legs of the bed. Create bedding using the candy paper. You can be as simple or as ornate as is warranted by time and sentiment.

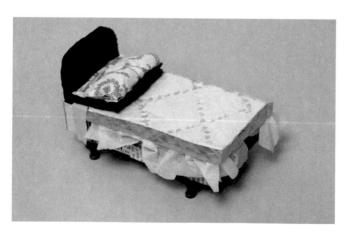

Painted rocks and bricks make excellent indoor tombstones.

MEXICAN SUGAR SKULLS

1 cup sugar

1 teaspoon meringue powder (available at baking stores)

1 teaspoon water

Plastic skull molds (each skull takes about ½ cup of sugar)

Sequins, colored frosting

Mix together sugar, meringue powder, and water with your hands until it feels like damp sand.

Pack into molds, carefully turn out onto a flat surface and let harden 24 hours before decorating.

Mexican Sugar Skulls

CONFECTIONERIES

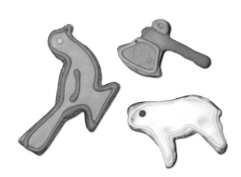

Confectionery

Spogs and spice, of taffied lollies
Syrupy honeyed candied sweeties
When life is serving the melancholies
Float me away on confectioneries.
—Gene Woodchuck

N ot all crafts involve utility knives, paste, and jangles. One craft uses a vastly different set of tools and materials, such as paring knives, almond paste, and jingles. I'm of course talking about the craft of baking. The best part of this craft is that when your project is complete you have a tasty treat you can eat instead of just another clothespin curler caddy.

GUMDROP WREATH

Instructions: Cut a 10-inch circle out of cardboard. Cut another smaller circle out of the center—it should resemble a halo. Glue one layer of gumdrops around. Hang anywhere that doesn't have mice, rats, or cockroaches.

BROWN BROWNS

YuM YuM

½ cup margarine

3½ cups powdered sugar

2 cups peanut butter

3 cups crushed Rice Krispies

1 pound semisweet chocolate chips, melted

Mix everything except the melted chocolate chips together. Roll into balls. Cover with melted chocolate. These are very yummy.

PEPPERMINT POPS LOLLIPOPS

Everyone enjoys seeing old people lick lollipops. It's good for their sinuses because the smell of peppermint oil wafts into their noses. With a lollipop in their mouth, they will appear youthful. (Recipe not included.)

RICH COCOA FUDGE

   1½ cups unsweetened cocoa

   6 cups sugar

   ½ teaspoon salt

   1½ cups whole milk

   12 ounces evaporated milk

   1 stick butter

   3 teaspoons vanilla

   Lightly buttered 9 x 12-inch pan

In a heavy 8-quart metal saucepan, mix together cocoa, sugar, and salt. Stir in both milks. Bring to a boil over medium heat, stirring constantly. Boil without stirring for about 50 to 60 minutes. Then stir in butter. Test by dropping a small amount of mixture into a cup of cold water. Test may be repeated 3 to 4 times until drop of fudge becomes a firm ball. Total cook time: about 65 minutes. Remove from heat, add vanilla, and beat at high speed until thick. (A hand mixer works best because you can feel the fudge becoming thicker as you beat.) It's done when mixture is thick, but can still be poured into prepared pan. Beat time: about 7 to 8 minutes.

After setting and cooling (about 40 minutes), cut into bite-sized pieces. (Nuts can be added just before pouring into pan.)

Courtesy of Ann Dinello.

OOEY GOOEY BARS

   1 box of pound cake mix

   1 stick butter (at room temperature)

   4 eggs

   8 ounces cream cheese (at room temperature)

   1 box powdered sugar

   1 cup pecan pieces

Preheat oven to 350 degrees F. Butter a 9 x 13-inch pan. In a large bowl, combine pound cake mix, butter, and 2 of the eggs. Spread mixture evenly into prepared pan. Combine cream cheese, the 2 remaining eggs, and two thirds of the box of powdered sugar (I use the same bowl). Mix well, then spread on top of first mixture. Sprinkle top with pecan pieces. Bake for 35 minutes. Sprinkle finished bars with remaining powdered sugar. That's it!

Courtesy of Sheila Harris.

FUN CLUBHOUSE COOKIES

The W.O.W. Cookie
(wheat-free, organic, and wondrous)

8 ounces walnut oil

¼ ounce good shake

1½ cups almond flour

1½ cups quinoa flour

1 cup fine masa harina (corn flour)

¼ cup tapioca flour

1 teaspoon salt

1 teaspoon baking soda

¾ cup white sugar

¾ cup loosely packed brown sugar

2 eggs, lightly beaten

2 tablespoons ground cinnamon

1 tablespoon ground ginger

4–6 good grates of nutmeg

1½ cups unsweetened cocoa

Take oil and shake and warm over low flame, constantly stirring as one would with pudding, never allowing it to boil, but bringing it to the edge, pressing the matter as you stir. Do this for at least an hour and a half, ideally 2 hours, until the oil is imbued with a greenish hue.

Preheat oven to 300 degrees F.

Mix flours in a bowl and add salt and baking soda, set aside. Mix sugars together in separate bowl.

Strain oil through a fine-mesh strainer, pressing all the while as you strain the still-hot oil into the sugar. Let caramelize as you cream together with hand mixer, then add eggs while slowly mixing. Add flour—slowly. When all is completely folded, fold in spices and cocoa. Mix thoroughly.

Make teaspoon size dollops to place on walnut-oiled stainless steel cookie sheet.

Bake 15 to 20 minutes, depending on how crisp you like them.

Courtesy of Jocelyn. Just livin' off the grid (don't use last name).

TOMAHAWK COOKIES

Use a tomahawk-shaped cookie cutter and an excellent butter cookie recipe. (I suggest this butter cookie recipe from *I Like You*.) Display these wonderful cookies at your next powwow.

SUSAN AND GRACIE'S AMAZING BUTTER COOKIES

- 1⅓ cups unsalted butter
- 1½ cups sugar
- 2 teaspoons pure vanilla extract
- 2 eggs
- 8 teaspoons milk
- 4 cups flour
- 3 teaspoons baking powder

Mix your dough and refrigerate overnight.

Roll dough out (I use 2 pieces of wax paper and a rolling pin, flour if needed) and use cookie cutters to make your shapes. Place on a greased cookie sheet and bake for 6 to 8 minutes.

Get your cookies to room temperature and refrigerate them overnight. Frost cookies the next day (see frosting recipe below) and place the cookies back in refrigerator for another night until the frosting hardens. You cannot eat enough of these.

FROSTING

- 1 box powdered sugar
- ¼ cup half-and-half
- 2 teaspoons pure vanilla extract
- 1 stick unsalted butter

Mix longer than usual. As seen in *I Like You*, page 230.

Cardboard Canoe

MY CARAMELS

1 cup sugar

¾ cup dark corn syrup

½ cup butter

1 cup heavy cream

½ cup nuts (pecans, walnuts, or black walnuts)

¼ teaspoon pure vanilla extract

Combine sugar, corn syrup, butter, and ½ cup of the heavy cream; bring to a boil, stirring constantly.

Add the remaining ½ cup heavy cream and cook slowly to very-hard-ball stage (260 degrees F on your candy thermometer) or use the cold water test method. Remove from heat; add nuts and vanilla. Pour into greased 8 x 8 x 2-inch square pan. Mark in squares when partially cool.

Cut when cold. Wrap caramels in squares of wax paper; keep in airtight container. Makes about 36 pieces.

A personal note: I oftentimes will stop cooking the caramels just shy of the 260-degree mark. When it sets up in the pan, you can scoop out spoonfuls of caramels, sort of like a soft caramel-sicle.

Courtesy of Cindy Selman.

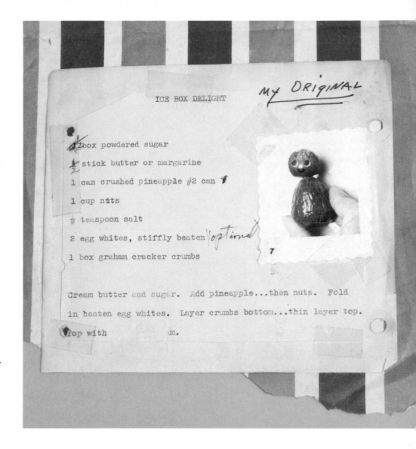

146

Simple and Sweet

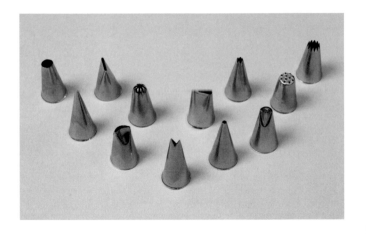

Jean's Quick Tip

I love using my frosting tips to add decorative trim to my cakes. Just practice first.

MY PLUMBER'S CHEESECAKE

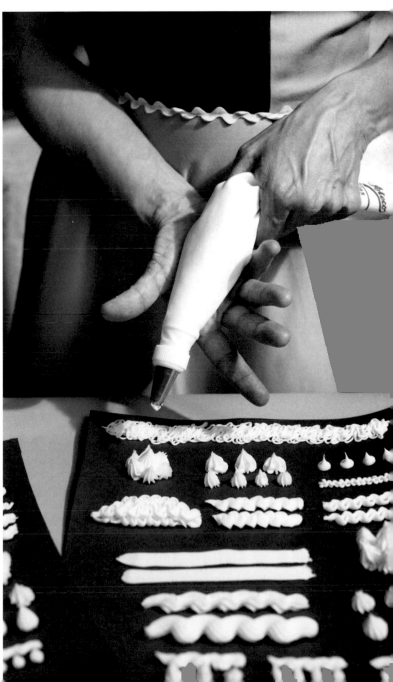

16 ounces cream cheese

1 cup sugar

5 eggs, separated

1¼ cups graham cracker crumbs

1 teaspoon cinnamon

1 pint sour cream

2 teaspoons pure vanilla extract

Soften cream cheese and add sugar. Beat well. Add yolks to cream cheese. Stiffen whites in separate bowl and then set aside. Add rest of ingredients to the mixture then fold in whites. Spread in 9-inch springform pan. Place in oven at 300 degrees F for 1 hour. Turn off oven and leave in for another hour. And then leave it for another hour with the door slightly open. Total suffering time: 3 hours. Chill for 3 hours to overnight.

Strawberry Sauce for Cheesecake

2 pounds strawberries, roughly chopped

½ cup to 1 cup sugar (to your liking)

2 teaspoons pure vanilla extract

2 tablespoons water

Put in pot on low to medium heat. Reduce down to a syrup-like texture. Can be served cold or warm. Spoon over slices of cheesecake.

Courtesy of Eric Russell.

BANANA PUDDING

4 eggs, separated

⅔ cup sugar

Salt

2 tablespoons cornstarch

3 cups whole milk

½ teaspoon pure vanilla extract

Vanilla wafer cookies

2 bananas, sliced

For Meringue

5 tablespoons sugar

1½ teaspoons pure vanilla extract

Beat the egg yolks. Add sugar, pinch of salt, and cornstarch. Add this mixture to the milk. Cook in a saucepan, stir constantly until mixture has thickened. Add vanilla.

Using an 8-inch square baking dish, layer the wafers and bananas. Stand vanilla wafers up and around the sides of the dish. Pour pudding over the vanilla wafers and bananas.

For the meringue, get a cookbook.

Celebrate!

Out of this world

rafting is considered to be a pasttime where one turns simple somethings into wonderful nothings. But did you know that crafting can also be mysterious and far out? Just imagine crafting in a galaxy from out of our craft dreams of tomorrow! Handmake the unexplainable! Fashion together, from everyday items around the house, the wonder of the incomprehensible!

Remember, when you enter the workroom, you are stepping into a craft time machine, so set the felt for the year unknown. Yarn and beads can take you anywhere you want to go. Popsicle sticks and glue can transport you to the land of marvel. Yes, crafting is the pastime of yesteryear we do today, but it is also the bygone, achieved in the here and now, that delivers us to the future, presently, and that is out of this world!

SPACE BALLS AND BLASTOFFS

Instructions: Combine coffee, sugar, and milk in a beaker. Shake ingredients for an extra light year. Pour contents over ice and serve with a straw. To create the accompanying Space Balls, cover round chocolate cake balls in shiny colored foil. The Space Balls photographed here are courtesy of the earthling Julie Le.

HOT PLATE

Instructions: Cover a box in tinfoil. Create flames using tissue paper. Use thumbtacks and a knob off an old timer to make the switches. Use the actual stove grate from your stove to create a realistic hot plate.

WAY OUT ROCKET

Instructions: Use an oatmeal box for the base and cardboard for the fins. Use batting or cotton to make the exciting blast-off smoke.

MACARONI ALIEN MASK

Instructions: Cut out the back portion of an empty pasta box. Cut small holes in the sides of the box toward the top. Run a length of string through the holes. Decorate the box in colors and shapes from another dimension.

Note: For larger skulls, look for manicotti boxes.

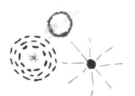

MARSHMALLOW STARS

Instructions: Using a needle, pierce the marshmallow with string and knot it at the end so the marshmallow won't slide off.

Rub glue on toothpicks and roll them through glitter.

Insert all the glitter-covered toothpicks into the marshmallow at various angles. Hang the star in a suitable place, preferably somewhere "out of this world."

You can color the marshmallow in food coloring mixed with water and you can cut the marshmallow into more of a ball shape.

The skill and coordination required for this project is minimal. I made this craft myself, so there was very little muscle involvement.

It's Showtime!

DIABOLICAL TINFOIL BRACELET
Instructions: It's alien to me. To fade construction paper, leave sheets in sunlight.

PLANETARIUM
Materials: You'll need an oatmeal box and a flashlight.
Instructions: Be an explorer and see if you can figure this one out on your own!

MUSTACHE AND WAND
To be a good magician you need to draw the attention of your crowd away from the part of you performing the trick. This is called "sleight of hand." This sort of manipulation takes years of practice. Here is a much easier way to create a distraction. Wear a large black mustache cut out from construction paper and wave around a home-made wand. This will also help you feel more in character, which makes it easier to lay down the magician's patter.

Instructions: Trace the mustache on cardboard, heavy poster board, or construction paper. Use a 15-inch dowel rod wrapped in silver tape to create the wand. Use black tape for the tip.

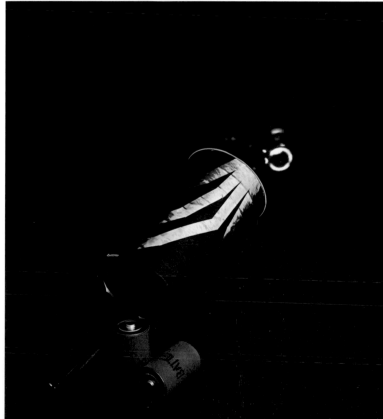

EGG CARTON BULGING EYES

Instructions: Cut out 2 side-by-side egg cup sections from an egg carton. Cut holes out for the eyes and make a space for the bridge of your nose. Poke holes in each side and pull a string through the holes.

ROCK CANDY

My experiment didn't work out because I didn't allow the sugar water to boil long enough. I think you can be a true scientist and explore a much better way to make your own recipe for this.

Materials: An empty jar, some string, a paperclip, and sugar and water.

VANISHING DENTED PING-PONG BALL

Instructions: If you find yourself in the possession of a crushed Ping-Pong ball, don't toss it away—repair it by dropping the ball into boiling water. Watch the dents vanish magically!!!

Crafting for Jesus

There can be no more righteous a reason to craft than crafting for Jesus. Even crafting for the sick pales tremendously in decency when held in the light of crafting in the name of our Lord. That said, crafting for profit can surpass crafting for Jesus in terms of virtuousness, depending on the profit margin. But why craft specifically for Jesus and not any of the other well-known prophets and/or sons of God? Is it because Jesus represents pure love and sacrifice? Not really. Perhaps it's because Jesus saw all mankind as equal? That could be true, but nothing really to celebrate, craftingly speaking. Maybe it has something to do with the miracle that somehow a Middle Eastern Jew possessed such Western European features? That certainly is worth celebrating, but it's not the reason. The reason is, of all the mystical entities we might pray to, Jesus just seems the most crafty. What with those hand-tooled sandals and artisan's smock, would it be much of a stretch to imagine any of the parables ending with Jesus resting on a stump and whittling a stick into the figure of a lamb? Jesus had the craftiest background of any deity. He was a carpenter. Can you picture Buddha operating a band saw? Even the miracles preformed by Jesus embrace the crafting ethic. Take turning water into wine. At its core, Jesus took a common substance, water, and miraculously turned it into something precious, wine. Not unlike a crafter taking something common, say a beer can, and miraculously turning it into an ashtray.

Crafters can identify with the story of Jesus, from his humble woodworking beginning, to his basic style and folksy wisdom, to his crafty, albeit grisly, demise nailed to the simple construction of two wooden beams in the shape of a cross. It might be difficult to place Jesus in modern times, but if we could, I don't think it would be too hard to imagine him at the center of a crafting circle, regaling the group with stories while adorning what once was a beer can and is now a simple, attractive ashtray that one just might choose to burn incense in.

The Ten Commandments of Crafting

I. Remember the crafting day, to keep it hobby.

II. Thou shalt not attempt crafting beyond thy intellectual capacity—a nitwit can't knit.

III. Thou shalt not craft graven images of thy neighbor's wife.

IV. Thou shalt remember to replace the glue cap so the top of the bottle doesn't dry out and then thou hast to get a pin to poke a hole but thy glue never really flows as well as it did before.

V. Thou shalt not fill envelopes with glitter and confetti and send them through the mail.

VI. Thou shalt remember that Popsicle stick crafts only have the illusion of being structurally sound.

VII. Thou shalt not force a mollusk out of its shell by boiling it alive but rather coax it out with a fork when making a shell necklace.

VIII. This craft book, which towers above all other craft books, is a jealous craft book. Thou shalt have no other craft books before it.

IX. Remember to honor thy crafting and pastimes for they are a great way to get your mind off all the damage that thou parents did.

X. Thou shall not covet thy neighbor's crafts, even though those crafts look like they are supposed to, and thouist crafts resemble a random pile of yarn.

MOSES' COMB HOLDER

Instructions: Place a comb over clear vinyl. Cut around the comb, allowing a small margin on all sides. Cut another piece of clear vinyl the same size. Seal all the ends, except the top, with colored tape. Decorate the cover with a brilliant cross also made of colored tape. Insert comb.

SHEPHERD'S BEARD

Instructions: To achieve this handsome shepherd's beard, save the hair from your hairbrush for at least six months. Apply to face using toupee tape, and fill in the bald spots with eye pencil.

Who am I?

I saw you in the craft room, and asked you to share your buttons and you snapped at me. I tried to show you my matchbook puzzle, which when assembled, completed an image of myrrh and you did not respond. I asked for your assistance when attempting to knot a tassel and you refused.

Who am I?

(It's Jesus)

165

MATCHBOOK PUZZLE

Instructions: Collect 6 matchbooks or 9, and assemble them into a rectangle. Cut a piece of construction paper that measures the same size as the boxes together. Create an image on the paper using paint or markers and then glue it onto the top of the boxes. After the glue has dried, separate the boxes using a utility knife. You can either leave the matches inside the box or replace them with small Cracker Jack–type surprises.

JESUS SANDALS

It has been said that you can't get to know someone until you "walk a mile in their shoes." Now you can understand all that there is to know about Jesus by creating these authentic sandals! Not to mention, because they are so fashionable, it wouldn't be surprising if you decided to keep them on for more than a mile.

Materials: Carpet scraps, floor mats, or worn-out tires.

Instructions: Ask a neighbor to trace your foot on the back of a carpet scrap. Recruit someone with some strength and experience with tools to cut the pattern out using a utility knife. Use an ice pick to pierce holes on either side of where your big toe will rest and run a leather shoelace through the holes, pulling forward the ends, and knot. You can wrap the excess string around your ankle or calf. The fit should feel snug, which is good because the laces will stretch. Now when you look back at the single pair of footprints on the sand you can say that they are both your and Jesus' footprints. Rejoice!

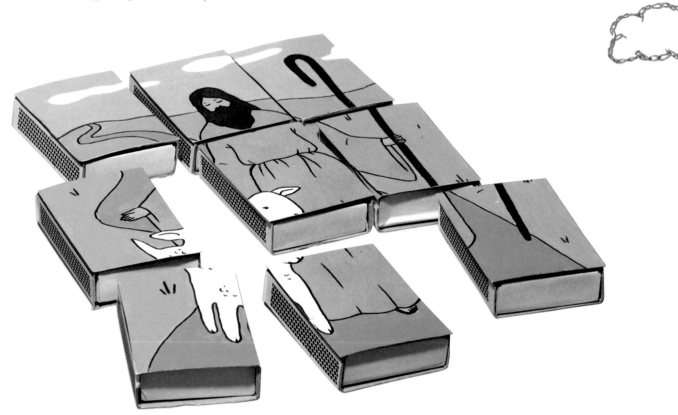

MATCHSTICK CROSS

Instructions: Cut a cross out of cardboard. Burn about 200 matches. There is a very specific way to lay the matches out but the guy who made this craft is in Alaska on a boat and can't be reached. This is a very popular craft so I am sure you can find the instructions at your local library.

JESUS BOX (SEE PAGE 112)

Instructions: Press the name "Jesus" into a box using thumbtacks. Can't really say for legal reasons, but you might need to wear a thimble on your "pressing" finger, or use a lady hammer because over time this activity can do some damage to the digits.

JESUS COINS (SEE PAGES 168–169)

Instructions: Cut a circle pattern out of cardboard. Use this pattern to cut felt pieces of the same size. Glue the felt pieces over the cardboard coin. This represents "sticking with Jesus." Any image you remember from the Bible can be recreated and placed on your coin.

MINIATURE BIBLES

Instructions: Take a sturdy piece of pitch-black construction paper and cut it into 5 x 6-inch pieces. Fold over in the middle to make the paper measure 5 x 3 inches. Round the corners of the cover and fill with white typing paper that is cut slightly smaller than the black paper. Print the words "Holy Bible" in gold on the outside and make curvy lines on the white paper to resemble Bible scriptures.

FRANCO'S CLOTHESPIN JESUS

Instructions: Construct your Jesus wall hanging using clothespins!

WOODEN SPOONS

Instructions: Paint Jesus on a wooden spoon. FUN!

BIBLE BOOKENDS

Instructions: Find 2 bricks that are shaped exactly like the Bible. Paint them black and write "Holy Bible" on the spine in gold.

10 LITTLE CROSSES

Instructions: Cut a piece of paper so that it measures 2 inches wide and 12 inches long. Fold it accordion style. Draw half of a cross so that the middle lines up with the fold. Cut along the outline. Open and you should have a row of crosses. Possibly.

BRAIDED HEAD OF THORNS

Instructions: Twist 2 long strips of leather around each other in a circular shape to fit your head. Tie smaller strips of leather around the circular shape to hold in place and create thorns.

JESUS DID IT!

QUEEN ESTHER

Instructions: Dip the tip of a wooden fork in glue and then glitter, creating a crown. Draw or paint a face onto the fork. Fashion a skirt out of construction paper and decorate the bottom of it.

DROP A DIME ON JESUS

Instructions: Bible stories look beautiful depicted on stamps. Use pinking shears to create the scalloped edge around your Bible picture to recreate that stamp look. Add the current stamp price and see if your local post office falls for it, but NEVER reveal where you got that idea.

HEAVENLY ANGEL FOOD CAKE

Instructions: To make the angel food cake, use 1 box of angel food cake mix. To make the wings (not pictured), ask a nine-year-old.

STAINED-GLASS-EFFECT CANDLES

Instructions: Mix 2 parts glue to 1 part water and set aside. Cut colored tissue paper into different shapes, also, set aside. Now run the tissue through the glue and apply it onto a short-stemmed goblet. Don't worry about over-lapping the pieces. Set aside. Using a marker, draw lines around the paper or even better, leave it plain. Pour a little water into the bottom of the glass. Place a small candle inside, and light.

STAR

Instructions: Gather a fistful of gold pipe cleaners. Bunch them, like uncooked spaghet-ti, and use another pipe cleaner to tie around the middle. Now unfold each pipe cleaner until it forms a star. Attach string and hang.

GLITTER HALO

Instructions: Cut a circle about the size of a plate out of sturdy cardboard, cover in glue, and apply gold glitter. Attach a band so you can wear it on your head.

ANGEL EYES AND MOUTH

Instructions: Cut eyelash shapes out of black felt and a mouth out of red felt. Ask an older man to create a tab for you out of paper and apply to the back of the angel mouth so you can hold it between your teeth to keep the mouth in place.

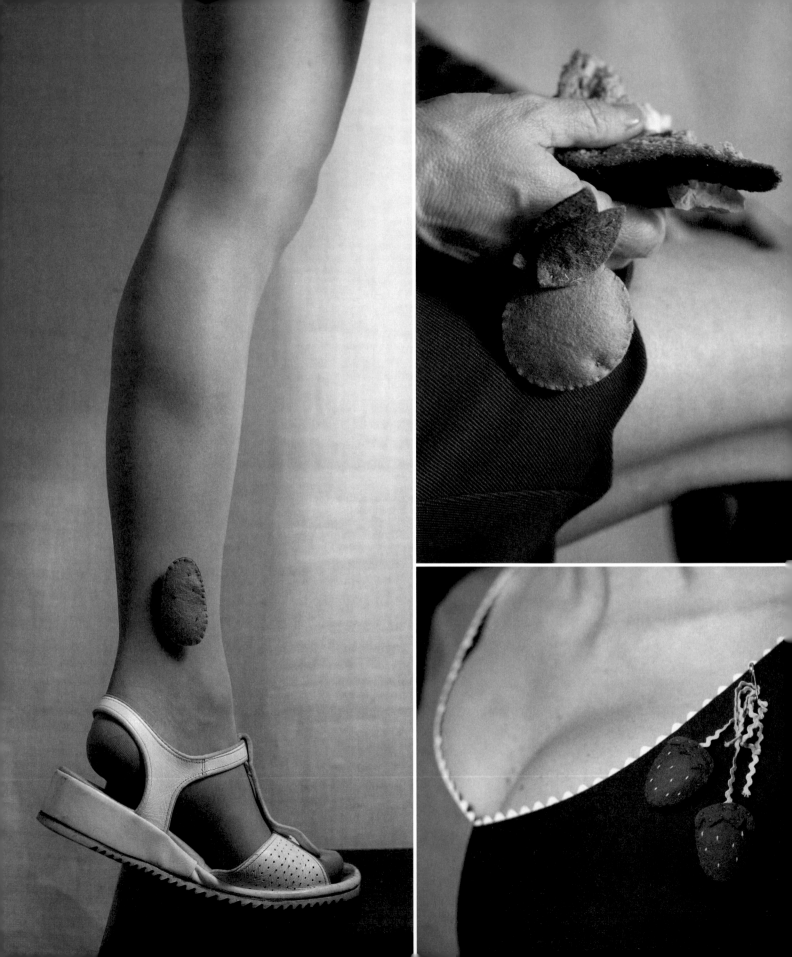

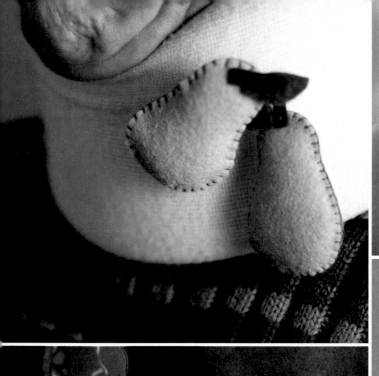

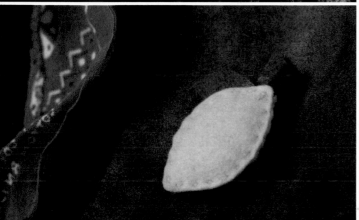

FELT FRUIT OF OUR LABOR PINS

Materials:

Scraps of colored felt

Safety pins or pin backs

Embroidery floss and needle

Cotton batting

Scissors

Instructions: Cut fruit shapes, leaves, and stems out of felt. Stitch around border using a blanket stitch-whip stitch or a running stitch, and leaving a small opening for stuffing. Stuff with cotton batting and stitch the hole closed. Attach leaves and stem with embroidery floss. Stitch or glue pin to back.

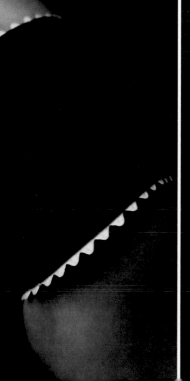

simple times

PEP TALK

Don't STOP NEVER HAVING NO SPIRIT!

At this point, you've tried a number of the wonderful crafts in this book and I bet you're thinking, "How come my projects don't look as good as the ones in the pictures? Maybe I'm not cut out for this?" Don't get down! First of all, comparing your crafts with the ones in this book is a no-win situation. Remember, the projects in this book were created by my professional team of underpaid outcasts and overworked misfits, and even though they worked in squalid conditions not dissimilar to those of the factory children of Victorian England, they have set a fairly high bar.

Secondly, and more important, did you know that inside your featureless well-worn husk is a creative you? "How can that be?" you might also ask. If we use the standard that everything is art and everyone is an artist, then there is a good chance that might include even you. You see, judging art is a matter of perception, and for every person who judges your project to be rubbish, there is another person who hasn't seen it. So don't be disheartened! Keep the glitter flying and the felt flowing! Because the only person you have to please is yourself, and let's face it, what do you know about art?

HAY BURNERS

f you have a pet, there are two things you know: one, you will never get that smell out of the couch; and two, they don't judge you. You could openly embezzle funds tagged for the local orphanage, and as long as you provide him with food and a warm place to sleep, "Hopscotch" will greet you with the same enthusiasm those orphans will greet Christmas morning with, at least until they realize there are not going to be any presents this year. And it is this unflinching naïveté that makes pets perfect to craft for. That is not to say that our pets will happily accept whatever you place in front of them. They may turn their nose up at the crocheted sweater vest or attempt to bury the miniature sombrero, but this has less to do with them consciously forming a negative opinion about your abilities, and more to do with the fact that the item isn't edible. Animals are always honest. They react in the moment and, unlike humans, they are not capable of backhanded compliments. They will not belittle your choices and they don't condescend. You are safe in crafting for your pet, and regardless of their reaction, you can be sure you will never hear such statements as, "If my aunt were alive, she'd probably enjoy this," or "Off the top of my head, I can't think of anything to do with this, but it's not for lack of trying," or "Has your therapist seen this?"

For me, when I talk about crafting for my pet I am talking specifically about rabbits. I have lived with one rabbit or another for many years now. There is much misinformation out there about rabbits and rabbit care. Perhaps one day I will work on a book just dealing with rabbits—are you listening, publishers of the Harry Potter series? I am willing to write a book solely about rabbits, no narrative, no amusing anecdotes, just dry rabbit facts, or are you tired of publishing blockbusters? Until that day, I will have to make do with including some crafty rabbit suggestions in this craft book. So here is a little taste of where the future of publishing is heading.

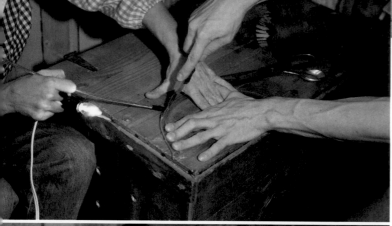

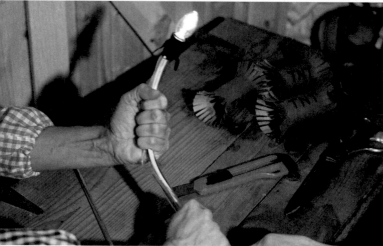

Rabbit Proofing Your Home

Rabbits love to chew. Their desire is insatiable, much like Japanese businessmen's craving for teenage prostitutes. Rabbits will chew furniture legs, bedspreads, clothing, drapes, high-heeled shoes, and baseboards. I was forced to nail a wooden two-by-four faux baseboard over my actual baseboard so my rabbit would chew the fake one and not the real one. I was renting the apartment and I wanted my deposit back. Unfortunately, I didn't account for the collective aroma that builds up after years of housing a rabbit in a small apartment, and I certainly didn't realize they would retain a deposit because of it.

But more than baseboards, or furniture, rabbits love to chew electrical cords. They enjoy the jolt. Like little junkies, they prance around the room gnawing on anything that has a current running through it. At the top of their list is a computer cord. Electrical cords must be protected so the rabbit can't get to them. Vinyl tubing that you can buy at the hardware store is best for this. Use a utility blade and split the tube lengthwise and then push the cord through. The tube will naturally close around the cord.

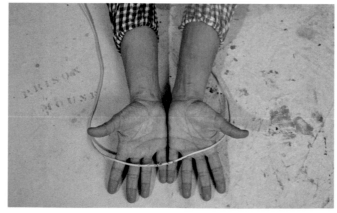

Rabbits enjoy the jolt from your cords.

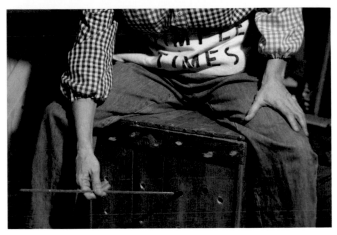

Hay needs to breathe. Drill holes in your hay storage box.

Rabbits love resistance. Protect your baseboards.

You can also encourage your rabbit to chew things that won't cut all the power to your appliances. Craft toys out of balsa wood for your rabbits to chew. Or if you want something slightly more ambitious, try crafting Dusty Dean Dynamite Sticks. Simply fill a toilet paper tube with treat hay, such as oat, and allow the hay to stick out the ends like a scarecrow. Rabbits love the fringed edges, and it's easier for them to pick these up with their teeth and toss around the room, hopefully keeping them busy long enough for you to rewire the lamps.

<u>KNOW YOUR HAZE</u>

Rabbits' primary food should be hay, and there are plenty
of varieties to choose from. Here is a guide to help you choose
the right dried grass for your little hay burner.

PREMIUM OAT BLEND
(KALI STALKS)

A righteous mixture of oat, barley, and rye, sure to
deliver a euphoric lunch. Flows down easy, won't clog
the throat. Sweet pungency. A supremely mellow
crunch that will give your rabbit the munchies.

ORCHARD GRASS HAY
(BUNNY BUD)

Soft, green, and fragrant grass hay with a delicate
note of citrus. A subtle yet stimulating chill chow.
Low on the harsh, but high on the soporific blur.
Makes dinnertime gently swing.

WESTERN TIMOTHY HAY
(KENTUCKY BLUE GRAZE HAZE)

A first-cut timothy grass hay with seed heads, a bit
sticky but bristling with resin. Rich earthy fragrance
with a bit of a kick. This ain't no ditch weed.

HAY MIXTURE
(SUPER STOMPIN' SHAKE)

A combo platter of bammy. A truly wacky hayhacky.
This supreme giggle chew is both stalky and crunchy,
packing the ultimate bunny buzz.

PREMIUM ALFALFA HAY
(SUPER STRAW KUSH)

Rich and leafy, this high-grade blend is not for the
faint-hearted rabbit. A fuzzy herbal aroma, this exotic
chronic feast delivers a fatty effect that is gastro-
blowing. Kala Kutchie Snootchie Mcboochies!

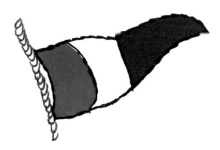

ELLIOT'S CILANTRO TREATS

1 banana

2 cups cilantro, chopped

½ cup pineapple, crushed (Do not drain juice. If you are us-ing canned pineapple, make sure it is just pineapple in juice. Do not use pineapple in syrup.)

1 cup oats

1 cup rabbit food pellets

You will need 2 baking sheets or stones lined with parchment paper.

Preheat oven to 325 degrees F. Puree banana, cilantro, and pineapple until consistency is smooth. Grind oats and pellets into a powder (a clean coffee grinder works best for this). Mix the puree, oats, and pellets together in a large bowl, and knead the dough until it is stiff enough to form a ball. Divide the dough in half, and place on baking sheets or stones, and roll to about ⅛ of an inch thick. Cut the sheets of dough into small squares (a pizza cutter works well). Bake for 30–35 minutes. Be careful not to brown the squares too much, especially if you are using baking sheets (metal sheets brown food faster than stones). Turn the oven off and let the treats sit in the warm oven for several hours. This last step is very important because it's what dries out and hardens the treats.

Hint: When you are rolling out the dough, put plastic wrap over it. This will prevent the dough from sticking to your rolling pin.

Courtesy of Katie Richardson.

CARDBOARD INDOOR RABBIT DWELLING

For a mini hutch, this is a good way to go because it has the textures rabbits love to gnaw on. Also, the material is fixed, and they love resistance. Leave the back or side open so your rabbit will have a way to enter. This rabbit dwelling pictured here was assembled using tubs of glue. Your challenge is to make this exact hutch, but without using glue or staples, which are not good for rabbits. Good luck.

Here are the top nine simple yet crucial things you must do to ensure your pet rabbit will be safe in your home.

1 Electrical wires must be covered or made inaccessible. Or better yet get rid of all electrical appliances including televisions. The Amish have been living this way for hundreds of years and they seem happy.

2 Toxic houseplants must be removed (many, if not most, common houseplants are toxic to rabbits). In other words no foliage in your home, including flowers, which, ironically, are the one thing that would have slightly combatted that gamey rabbit smell.

3 Flat, no-pile, nonskid carpeting is needed to give rabbits traction and a place to run and leap. After switching out all your carpeting, why not remove the furniture to really allow them to cut loose?

4 Rabbits love to chew against resistance. Woodwork is a big favorite for many rabbits. If you live in an old building, assume there is lead paint under your current paint, and prevent rabbits' access and chewing. The easiest way to do this is to gut your place entirely, all the way down to the studs! Put up new drywall and crown molding, and cover with responsible non-rabbit-killing paint.

5 Prevent rabbits' access to toxic substances you may use around the house—especially insecticides and rodenticides. Cleaning chemicals (particularly those containing limonene or pine oils) may also be harmful to rabbits. You will need to toss out all your cleaning supplies, including your broom. Brooms are a chewing hazard. This is unfortunate, because what's not covered in rabbit droppings will be dusted with hay, so now that you own a rabbit your desire to clean will never be more burning.

6 Reclining chairs are particularly hazardous. Rabbits can climb, unseen, into the mechanism and can be crushed when someone leans back. All comfy chairs must go!

7 Prevent rabbits' access under the bed—rabbits love to chew the filmy fiberglass covering that is tacked on the underside of the box spring. This can be lethal. The downside is, you will be resting in a sleeping bag on a flat rug. The upside? You have a rabbit!

8 Put away human snacks and pet foods. Rabbits should not ingest chocolate (or any other high-carbohydrate food), and should not ingest dog or cat food. It's about time you and your dog went on a diet, isn't it?

9 Be careful with toys that can wrap around a rabbit's neck (such as a large-sized slinky). The rabbit can panic in an attempt to escape, and can seriously hurt himself. Even chewed-up towels with holes in them can be hazardous if the bunny's head gets caught. It's just best to not have toys. You have a rabbit now and that should be the focus of your joy!

Unreturnable Gift Giving

Throughout human history, gift giving has been a long and wonderful tradition. Whose heart is not warmed by the memory of the Kula ring being passed on during the Moka exchange by the tribes of Papua New Guinea? Or the generosity of the Kwakiutl practiced at the potlatch ritual? Certainly it is hard to deny that fond fuzzy feeling when reminiscing about all those great blankets the white settlers gave the American Indians. Today, humans continue to exchange gifts as a show of friendship or adoration or desire for a promotion. For most of us, gifts mean store-bought items that usually make up in quality what they lack in that crude adorable rusticness. Anybody can give a mass-produced item, but in the good old days,* thoughtful handmade items were exchanged, such as knitted wearables, charmingly carved tchotchkes, and smoked meats as expressions of love, friendship, and/or meat. Even today, we can still capture that old-fashioned cozy tradition of gift giving by hand-making our gifts.

But why go to the trouble of giving a handmade gift? Is it the fact that it's much cheaper than buying something that a person actually wants? No, probably not. Does it have something then to do with the fact that making a gift is a good way to get rid of the odds and ends you don't have the energy to toss out? For argument's sake, let's say no. How about the idea that crafting a gift gives the illusion that you are "artsy," or doesn't require you to leave the house to shop, or is a good opportunity to practice doing something you are hoping one day you will be good enough at to turn a profit on? Some valid points, maybe, but the simple reason we are settling on is this: when you give something you made to someone, they know that you are giving to them a piece of you, and they understand that you have presented them with you. Simple!

* Regardless of research, it appears impossible to pin down the actual dates of "the good old days," but I believe it can be said with some certainty that "the good old days" are probably, at least, the days before this one.

Gifts for a Man You Are Dating Who Is at Least 18 Years Older Than You

MISS EGYPT SHOP TOWEL HOLDER

Instructions: Wrap a roll of blue shop towels in washcloths. Use a scouring pad for the hair and cut feet out of sandpaper. Draw on the pretty eyes. He won't need anything else in his shop.

LIL' HOT FOOT FIRE STARTER

Instructions: Make a shoe out of newspaper using tape. Apply rows and rows of matches from a matchbook.

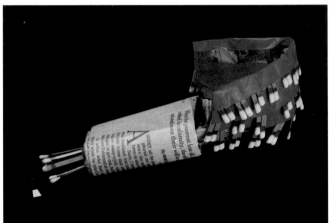

Gift for a Nudist

SEAT SHIELD

Instructions: Make a doily or decorate a piece of washable fabric a nudist can carry wherever they go to use to sit on when visiting family or friends with nice couches.

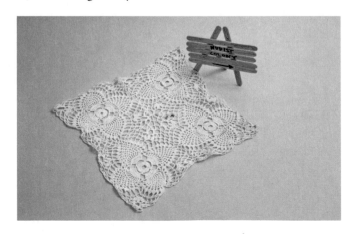

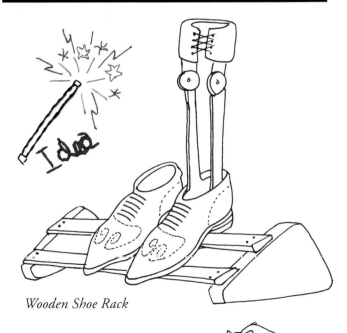

Wooden Shoe Rack

Gift for the
World Traveler
LUGGAGE TAG

Gifts for Mom
"I CAN'T FIND MY KEYS"

Instructions: Attach an attractive bell onto Mother's keys so when she is digging in her bag she will hear them.

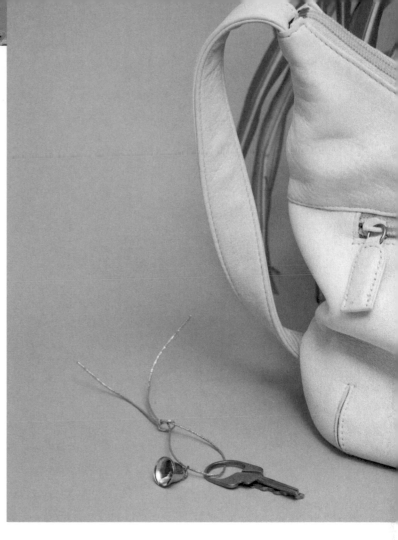

BUTTON AND BUCKLE BOOK

Instructions: Gather all your mother's random buttons and buckles. Sew the buttons and buckles onto 8 x 10-inch pieces of stiff cardboard and fasten the backs with a knot. Attach all the pages of cardboard together to make a book. Decorate the pages and the outside.

PENNY BOOKMARK (SEE INSTRUCTIONS ON PAGE 39)
Note: Count the pennies and your dollars will follow.

Root Beer Brown

Brown Brown

**Gifts for Someone You Are Dating
Who Is at Least 18 Years Younger Than You**

ROOT BEER BROWN

Instructions: Make a stuffed cat. Make eyes out of felt.

BROWN BROWN

Instructions: Make a small stuffed dog. To make the four-leaf clover, cut the shape out of green felt.

ELEPHANT (SEE PAGE 149)

Instructions: To make the elephant's tail use some household string and fray the end.

GINGHAM BOTTOMS

What girl wouldn't love a pair of gingham bottoms?

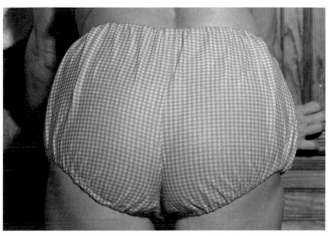

Animal Eyes

and Tongues

Tin Can Characters

Gift for the
Professional Golfer
POMPON GOLF CLUB COVERS

Gift for the
Single Working Woman
BLUE JEAN BOOK COVER WITH POCKET FOR POMPON PENCIL

Gift for All Ages
MONEY CANS

Instructions: Cover cans with construction paper and felt. Turn them into your favorite characters.

Gift for the Bookworm
BOXY BOOKMARKS (SEE NEXT PAGE)

Instructions: Use old cereal and toothpaste boxes for these. Cut them into strips and decorate.

Gift for Dad
SCRAP STAMP BOX (SEE PAGE 191)

Instructions: Cut up your favorite wrapping paper and glue to the outside of a box. Outline the pieces in black marker.

Gift for an Older Sister

BANDANA BOX

Instructions: Paint the inside and outside of a cigar box. Decorate as you wish. Fill with bandanas and handkerchiefs.

JEAN'S CORNER

Gene and I always exchange homemade gifts. But one time I asked for a dishwasher. I even had one all picked out from Clawson's Appliances, but Gene insisted on making me one instead, reassuring me that his choice had nothing to do with the price tag of the one at Clawson's. He claimed it would be much more charming if, instead of buying me a dishwasher, he would just cobble some scraps together from the shed—random plywood, pieces of an old furnace and part of a gutter—and call it a dishwasher. Guess what, it doesn't clean dishes. It barely holds water, but Gene keeps saying it's the thought that counts, and I got to believe him. So I still wash my dishes in the sink, but now I have a homemade something I can store pots and pans in, and I suppose that's something.

JEAN'S HOMEMADE GIFT SUGGESTIONS

A cutting from your garden, a hand-painted pot, pressed flowers, a decorative case for eyeglasses, a fresh baked loaf of bread, home-brewed dandelion wine for the outdoorsman.

Gifts for the Private Nurse

FLAVORED OIL

Instructions: Collect small bottles, fill with olive oil and dried chili peppers and seal with cork.

SEEDS FOR HER OWN GARDEN

PERSONALIZED HANKY

Note: So she won't confuse it with one of yours.

SWEEP ME OFF MY FEET BROOM COVER

(SEE PAGE 279)

Instructions: Make a pattern by tracing the bottom part of your broom onto a piece of paper. Cut felt using this pattern. Sew or glue the seams together and scallop, or use pinking shears, along the bottom edges. Slip over your broom. Use a strip of felt to wrap around the cover so it will stay on the broom.

Gifts for Your Favorite Aunt
PENCIL CAN

Instructions: Use a sugared peanut can (although any can with a plastic top will probably do), and punch holes in the lid with a hole punch. Decorate can with paper, trim, rubber stamps, sequins, stencils, fringe, or anything you like.

Gift for a Brother
SMELLY BALSAM SACK

Eyeball it.

Gift for an Ill Person
BOUNCE BACK BOX

Make a bounce back box for a shut-in. Wrap a few small gifts, write a get-well message or Bible scripture note, and place the gifts inside the bounce back box and take it to your shut-in.

Gift for a Missionary
NATURAL-LOOKING PENCILS

Instructions: Wrap unsharpened pencils tightly in wood grain shelf paper.

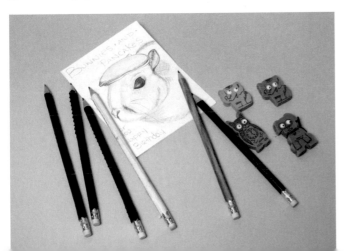

Gift for the Grieving
SMOKED HAM

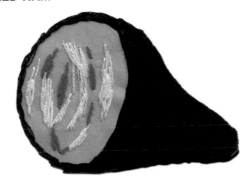

Boxes Are Handy

Busy Work for Little Hands

Gingham

SHUT-INS

I nfirmity, much to the surprise of sprightly crafters, is actually a wonderful opportunity to craft. These people might be shut-ins, but they are not shut-outs! Yes, the bedridden are generally in a weakened state, but nobody has more time on their hands than they do. Boredom is often the number-one enemy of the bedridden, at least until whatever the "condition" that is keeping them in bed turns south, and then boredom is a blessing. The bedridden are happy to engage in any activity that will pass the time. Also, crafting from a large comfy bed is something even the most vibrant crafters aspire to. There are a couple of things to keep in mind when "feeble-crafting." The crafts should be simple. They should be crafts that can be completed in many small sessions and for which untimely interruptions, say an unscheduled nap or a narcotic haze, won't impede the final product. The craft should not require any dangerous tools, glues, or chemicals. Nobody—bedridden or otherwise—wants to wake from a slumber to find themselves adhered to a bedpan. Crafting can be a wonderful hobby for the bedridden: it keeps their mind focused, it provides a way to creatively pass the time, and there is no pressure on the final outcome of the craft because when the end is looming, the process is always more important than the product.

1 YESTERDAY'S NEWSPAPER SCUFFS

Instructions: Slippers will protect your feet on those rare occasions you get out of bed, and since you are so rarely out of bed, newspaper will be a fine material because these slippers will not get much wear.

2 ASPIRIN CHART

Instructions: Staple individual aspirin tablet packages onto the bottom half of a piece of stiff cardboard. Decorate the top half and hang on your wall. These aspirin should be for the shut-in only.

3 SILENCE SIGN

Instructions: Every door should have a privacy sign. Make one from cardboard and attach a string so it can dangle from a doorknob. Decorate according to mood.

4 DECORATIVE CRAP CADDY

Instructions: Don't just bring your stool sample to the doctor's office in any old sack—create your own special crap caddy. Decorate a plastic container with adhesive stars.

5 CHEER UP BIRD (SEE PAGE 217)

Instructions: Take 2 birds that you have cut out of construction paper that are exactly the same size. Cut a slot at the tail end and near the breast bone of the birds. Paste the birds together. Slide 2 pieces of pleated crepe paper through the slots you cut. Decorate bird with eyes and by writing "He Careth for You" on one side. This will cheer up any bed tray and will stimulate appetite.

6 NOTEPAD

Instructions: Staple blank pieces of colorful paper to the top end of a stiff piece of cardboard. Attach a pen to a long string and tape it to the back of the board.

7 BED TRAY MATS

Instructions: Easy to clean place mats are always a plus. Decorate a piece of sturdy cardboard with trim and stars and then seal with clear packing tape.

8 TEA BELL

Instructions: (As seen in *I Like You,* page 162!) Drop a tooth or quarter or beer cap into a metal can with a tight-fitting lid. Cover the can and rattle it when you need help.

9 HEATING PAD COVER

Instructions: Cover your heating pad with random colorful cotton balls.

10 TISSUE BOX

Instructions: Cover your tissue box with colorful tape.

JEAN'S CORNER

After Gene had recovered from his illness I had to make sure everything in his sick room was cleaned and aired out.

I took his mattress and rugs and pillows and books and toys and put them out in the open air to be sunned for about eight hours. Everything else I washed with soapy scalding water.

Greetings Little Shut-In

Presenting the right gift to those who are bedridden can prove to be difficult. Because these people have such a variety of physical and emotional needs, pinpointing the perfect present can sometimes be frustrating. Possible gift choices might seem obvious, like a bathrobe or slippers, but practical doesn't always mean perfect, and taking a "gift gamble," might just be the spark that gets them through another day. When giving a person who is bedridden a handmade craft, there are a few general tips you can follow. Whatever you craft, use bright colors. Not only does this cheer up the room a bit, but it helps to counteract the shut-in's sallow ghostly pallor. "Stationary," "motionless," and "static" are good words to remember when crafting for shut-ins. A craft that conveys freedom of movement, such as a wind chime or a bead curtain, too often is a reminder of better times and runs the risk of belittling the shut-in's sedentariness. Nobody confined to a mattress wants to be mocked by the loosey-goosey at-

tributes of a tassel. Also, craft using fragrant items such as pine or cedar to help combat that all too familiar "shut-in smell."

The next time you visit the bedridden, take a chance, and bring him a handcrafted gift. This will show them that you are thinking about them and giving something of yourself. Also, a handcrafted gift is nonreturnable, saving them the frustration of getting a pricey store-bought gift that they aren't crazy about and would love to return for cash but can't because they do not have the ability to leave the room.

REAL HOB KNOB GLASS CANDLES

Instructions: Glue dried peas to a glass. Paint the outside, including the peas. Insert a candle. This tactile craft is also terrific for the blind.

"MY ONLY FRIENDS"

Instructions: Decorate nuts found in the woods. Dress with googly eyes to make them look alive. You can use a pinecone to make a chandelier to dangle over your new buddies.

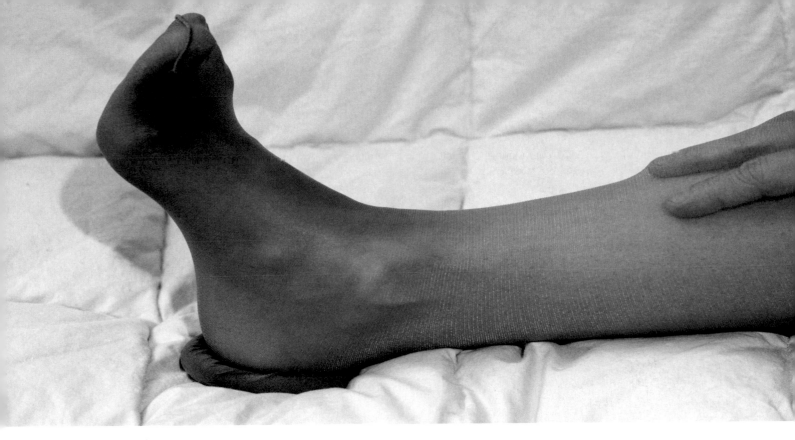

"HEELING" DONUT

Instructions: If your heel (or elbow) is infected, take a stocking and, starting at the top, roll over and over right down to the toe so that it resembles a donut. Place this under the infected area.

VANITY FOOT STOOL COVER

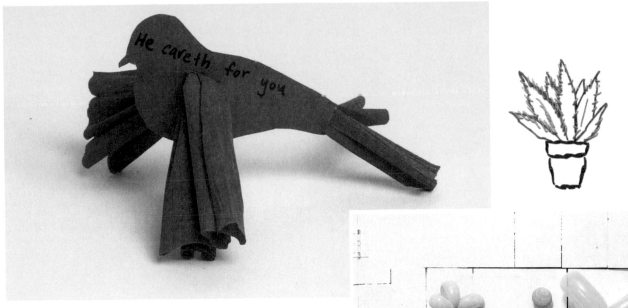

Cheer Up Bird

SHUT-IN SHUFFLE SLIPPERS

Instructions: If you don't knit, ask a lady who does and have her knit you some pretty house slippers. If you are a man she should use dark color yarn, for a woman maybe a light color or curry color.

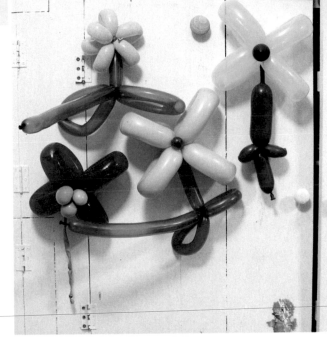

GENE'S CORNER

I was out of commission a few months back after I fell off the shed while trying to trap a squirrel with a rake. I mostly just needed to rest, but Jean kept dragging my bedding out to the yard for God knows what goddamn reason. I was forced to convalesce on a stool while waiting for my goddamn mattress to return. When it did come back, my bedding smelled like damp leaves. I thought I was never gonna get better.

Busy Hands for Little Work

Bandana!

Fireside Storytelling

One cold early winter morning while nestled under my enduro-fleece microfiber electric heating blanket with the switch set to cozy and considering the many ways I had benefited since embracing a simpler life, I heard a loud crash from downstairs. I quickly realized, that other than me, the house should be empty. The cooking staff doesn't arrive until late morning, and I was forced, regrettably, to let my housekeeper go due to her inability to maintain a sparkle on my "float down the stairs" transporter chair. Alarmed, I sat up in bed to take a better listen. At first nothing, and then footsteps! Distinctive footsteps growing louder across my black-market Brazilian rosewood floors in the foyer, and then over my hand-spun baby camel rug from Makalu also in the foyer and then pausing at the bottom of the stairs. Slowly and methodically the steps continued up the staircase. My first thought was, "Why did I fire Carmencita?" Certainly her duties as my employee would require her to "take a bullet," as they say. Are not housekeepers similar to Secret Service men in that they must give their life for their employer? But now, because of her ineptitude with a rag and silver polish, I become the primary target! There will be no spunky Mexican buffer! The mysterious figure paused at the top of the stairs for a moment—exhausted, I'm sure, from having to actually climb them—and moved toward my room. I froze with terror as the doorknob jiggled and the door swung open. Then, in a blur, I reached for my gold-plated Smith & Wesson and fired. The shadowy shape clothed in a colorful open-sleeved Puebla blouse and a flower-patterned pica skirt crumbled to the floor. After the smoke cleared, it had appeared that in the abrupt dismissal of Carmencita, I had neglected to inform her. As she mumbled something in Spanish, which had the tone of a vulgarity but I'm sure was an apology, it occurred to me that the two of us would always fondly share this memory of when I gave Carmencita the opportunity to completely fulfill her housekeeping obligations.

What just happened? Why is this compelling story included in a book on crafting? You've just been introduced to the craft of storytelling! Storytelling has a long history. From the time man had discovered the words "the end," he has been spinning yarns. Stories have been handed down from generation to generation and were used

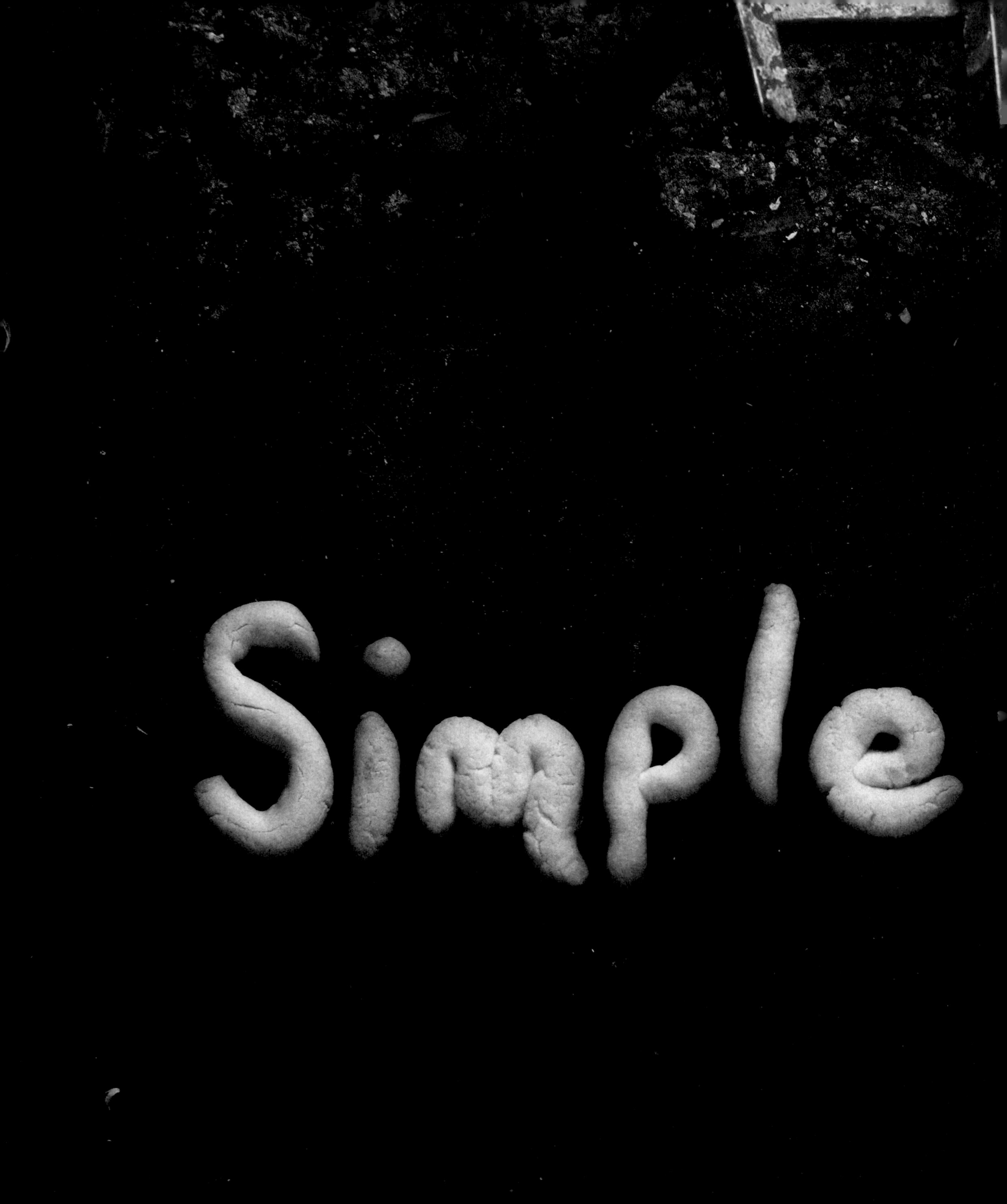
Simple

as a way to inform, entertain, or make excuses as to why you were late. There are numerous ways to enrich your storytelling—punctuating thoughts with long pauses, arching an eyebrow and nodding when a point has been made, stroking a beard that doesn't exist—but nothing enhances storytelling quite like fire. Fire is a warm, comfortable way to draw listeners in before you begin all that talking. Since man first discovered fire, he has been compelled to sit around it and tell stories. Fire had an almost magical quality that suggested anything was possible. Early on, man even believed that fire was a god that had to be fed with animal sacrifices in order to burn brightly. Today we have evolved a long way from this ridiculous notion of a "fire god" and now rightfully understand God to be a bearded being who lives amongst the clouds and hates Jews and homosexuals.

Sawdust Fire Starters

FIRESIDE SIT-UPON

Instructions: Sit-upons are good to rest on so that we can avoid getting our bottoms stained or wet. To make one, use about a dozen double-page sheets of newspaper. Fold each sheet in half and then in half again until you have strips about 2 inches wide and 24 inches long. Make sure the strips are as flat as they can be. Lay 6 strips down on the floor about 3 inches apart. Weave the other strips in and out. You are now making the mat. Fasten the loose ends by doubling each one back and over the closest strip and tuck the end under the strip. You should do this to all four sides. This is how they taught us to make sit-upons in Girl Scouts, but today I worry less about the "weaving" and the "tucking" and rely on a whole lot of glue.

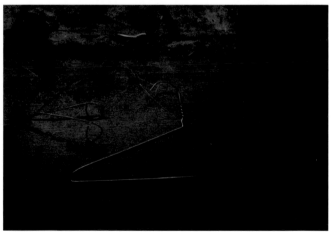

CHARCOAL HOLDERS

Instructions: Cut a hanger so you have one long wire. Bend the wire in half, folding each end back 2 inches. Grip at the top of the holder and squeeze to grasp charcoal.

Tips to Becoming a Better Storyteller

1 SETTING THE ATMOSPHERE

As mentioned earlier, a fire will go a long way toward setting a warm storytelling mood. There are other things you can do to prepare your listeners to be storied. Sit on a stump. Regardless of what you are doing—fishing or mapping genomes—it is going to seem more folksy when resting on a tree stump. If there is no tree stump available, go down on one knee in the same way a lumberjack might when he is about to propose. Another nice touch for setting a mood is whittling while you tell your tale. This way you can emphasize story points with the flick of your knife—not to mention, if the end of the story coincides with the completion of say, your wooden turtle, you are sure to impress.

2 GET THEIR ATTENTION!

In storytelling jargon, this is known as "starting with a zinger!" Begin your story with a sentence that will immediately grab hold of your listener's ears like a surly nun in a Catholic school. Here are some examples:

"There was a time, he exclaimed to his freshly assembled war council, when I wore nothing but denim!"

"As the car came to a violent skidding halt, causing gravel to be propelled from the wheels like tiny rocks shot out of a tire cannon, Tanya reuttered her shocking revelation to Toby, 'Chad Chambers already asked me to go steady.' "

"What began like any ordinary camping trip soon ended that way as well."

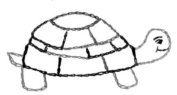

3 BUILD TO A THRILLING CLIMAX

Your story should take listeners on a rousing roller-coaster ride with the tension and excitement ramping up throughout the tale and peaking toward the shocking conclusion. The way to achieve this is to contradict the current action, whatever that may be. For example, if you establish a pontoon full of celebrating seniors, send it over the falls. A handful of clowns in a clown car should result in an eleven clown car pileup. A pleasant romp in the woods should be followed by the words, "accosted by wolves." Whenever stuck for an action to follow your established action, simply have it "burst into flames."

4 THE TWIST

Every good story needs a twist, otherwise known as the "The call is coming from inside the house!" moment. The key here is to remember: the bigger the twist, the more implausible it can be. Nobody is going to expend energy checking facts once they discover the ice pick belongs to Giles, the mute stable boy!

The craft of storytelling has a long rich tradition, so light a fire, pull up a stump, and start talking. And remember, if you get stuck and are not sure how to proceed, have your main characters erupt into a blazing inferno. Your listeners will love you for it.

Fireplace Hot Dogs on a Rake

Teenagers Have A Lot of Pain

Nothing strikes fear in the heart quite like the word "teenager." According to Stanford-Binet's *Catalogue of Terms That Instill Terror,* "teenager" falls just between "colonoscopy" and "ethnic cleansing."

Teenagers do not respond to authority; just watch the expression on one of their faces after you've politely asked him to chase the raccoons out of your attic. Unlike small children, teenagers are no longer easy to manipulate through threats. Whether or not you have the energy or legal latitude to actually follow through, youngsters have a difficult time accurately assessing the actual danger of your ranted warnings and will yield to your desires. Teenagers, on the other hand, will call your bluff, or worse, ignore you completely, forcing you to do some pretty despicable things just to prove a point. What's worse, according to the renowned amateur golfing clinical psychologist Dr. Francis Anthony, "If there is one thing I know, it's two things: Adolescence, with all its repugnance, starts earlier and stays later than any sane parent can tolerate; and never start a round of golf behind a foursome of ladies."

But why does this aggressive and rebellious behavior associated with adolescence take root? Teenagers are dealing with all sorts of changes to their bodies: awkward growth spurts, acne, unfortunate hairstyle choices. But the most devastating changes are hormonal. This surge in testosterone, estrogen, and progesterone turns our innocent angels, much like werewolves during a full moon, into sex-starved, drug-fueled carnivores who prowl the night.

So how can we exhausted, weary crafters combat the abhorrent behavior of these postpubescent buccaneers? Activity. Keep their hands busy and their genitals will follow. But not just any activity, because although it has been said that idle hands are the devil's workshop, when it comes to teenagers, both idle and active hands are the devil's workshop. For instance, let's say your teenager is keeping his hands good and busy rolling a "doobie" or fondling the neighbor's daughter or setting a boat on fire. One would assume, given the "devil's workshop" idiom, that at least this teenager's active recreation will keep further demons at bay. But we all know where this evening is headed, and it's not going to end until the quiet of the night is pierced by screaming sirens. Let's face it; pretty much everything an adolescent does with his hands is the devil's workshop. Except for crafting. But why does crafting have such a positive influence over this dungaree-clad rebel menace?

Crafting stimulates many areas of the reckless brain. Sensory overload is the key to control. Crafting requires shape and pattern recognition, construction mobility, color palate perception, and hand-eye coordination. But most important, when all else fails, crafting will keep even the most impetuous teenager in check by narcotizing him with excessive glue and paint fumes into a courteous drone.

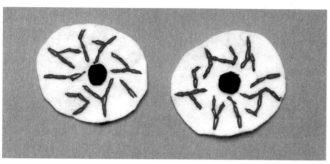

FELT EYEBALLS

Instructions: These eyes will punch up your skullcap or add character to your jean jacket.

TAMPON GHOST

Instructions: Self-explanatory.

GEM SWEATER

Instructions: Have someone knit you a miniature sweater, and then apply your favorite post earrings.

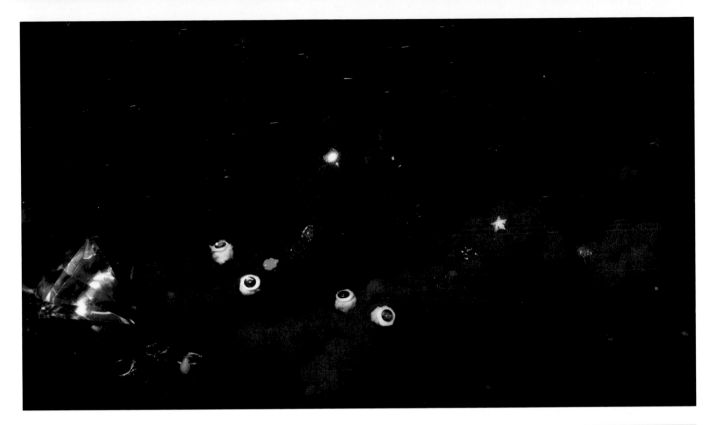

GEMINI GEM WORM

Instructions: Take a long string of pompons and fold it over. Add gem rings and a pair of eyes. Put the rings you wear the most toward the bottom of the worm so they are easy to wiggle it off.

GLITTER BOX AND PAPER FLOWERS

Instructions: Cut stacks of circles out of paper. The bigger the circle the more layers you need. The thinner the paper the more layers you will need. Let's face it: you are going to need a lot of layers. Stack the layers together and connect through the center with a pipe cleaner. Next, start with the top centerpiece and crunch the ends toward the center. Work your way down the layers, crunching as you go.

Glitter tips: When covering crafts in glitter, first apply a base coat of a matching color paint. Outline your design with a black marker. Add a layer of glue. Pour the glitter on while the glue is wet. Dust off excess. After it dries, use a high-gloss spray varnish to seal. The reason you should use a matching base coat is that if the glitter comes off in a smaller area you won't be able to tell.

SECRET TREASURE BOX

Instructions: Decorate the outside of a box you are fond of. Fill this secret box with irreplaceable sentimental treasures and keep in a safe place.

BANG IT OUT

Instructions: For an instant hairstyle in seconds, attach a pair of bangs to the inside of a hat, bonnet, or scarf and apply to your head.

DRAWSTRING BAGS

Instructions: Add your name to old drawstring bags.

GENE'S CORNER

I am all behind this teenagers and crafting. I think it's great! Anything that keeps them from hiding bags of dog crap in my work boots is all right by me. Christ, I got to get a lock for that shed. I remember when I hit puberty around the fourth grade. The hair started on my upper lip, and it didn't stop until my ass cheeks looked like a couple of woodchucks scampering down a hole. I felt a lot of confusion during those years, from you know, let's say nine to my early forties. I wish I had crafting to turn to in those times. I probably would have lit a lot less public property on fire.

WIZARD DUCK COSTUME

Instructions: Make your own clothing line for the stuffed animals that you have outgrown. To make the rain cloud, add gray paint to the cotton ball, dangle from a wire and attach to a spindle.

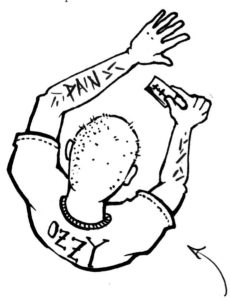

TEENAGERS HAVE A LOT OF PAIN.

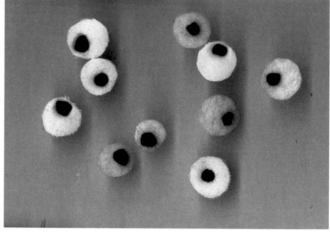

Eyeball It---

Googly Eyes

TRAVEL LUNCH BOXES

Instructions: Decorate old lunch buckets to bring on your next trip. These are terrific for storing your prescriptions or craft supplies.

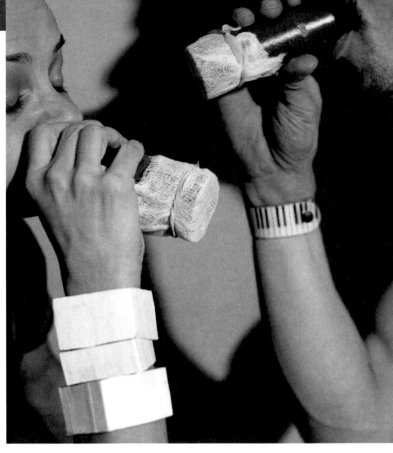

dingbat

KAZOO

Instructions: Learn to play music instantly without Instruction. Wrap a piece of wax paper around the opening of one of the ends of a toilet paper tube. We used gauze, which doesn't work. Make sure the paper is good and tight and stretch a rubber band around the end of the tube to hold the wax paper in place. Using a pencil, punch a hole through the tube about an inch from the end that the wax paper is covering.

EIGHTY-EIGHTS BRACELET WITH BREAKAWAY SLEEVE

Instructions: Using a pen or marker, draw piano keys onto a leather band and add a snap. Or you can use a wide rubber band and avoid the snap. To make the breakaway sleeve, tear a sleeve off a favorite shirt or blouse. Add elastic to the top.

DISPOSABLE NEWSPAPER-PRINT APRON

CRAZY JEANS

Instructions: Teenagers love blue jeans and hot dogs. Glue or sew your favorite patches to your favorite jeans. To be really bold, add rickrack to the bottom of the pant legs.

WHEELCHAIR BACKPACK

This is a terrific idea for a teenager in a wheelchair.
Instructions: Decorate a backpack to hang on the back of your wheelchair and hold artist supplies. Lay your backpack on a worktable. Gather all the trim and pompons you can stomach and arm yourself with a glue gun, then go to town.

POMPON CANISTER

Instructions: Paint an oatmeal canister and then wrap a string of pompons around the body and adhere with either thumbtacks or glue. Do as many rows as you like.

This is excellent to keep secret letters and notes in.

Construction Paper and Rickrack Banner

TEENAGERS HAVE A LOT OF PAIN BELT

Instructions: Using a wood-burning kit, inscribe "Teenagers Have a Lot of Pain" into a belt and wear it around your waist or wrap around your favorite tree trunk.

"I CAN'T DO ANYTHING RIGHT" BOX

Instructions: Carve your feelings into a wooden box.

ANGST JOURNAL

Instructions: Every teenager needs a journal to keep track of their feelings, so they can look back years later to see how unreasonable they were. Also makes a good reference guide when visiting a therapist in later years.

239

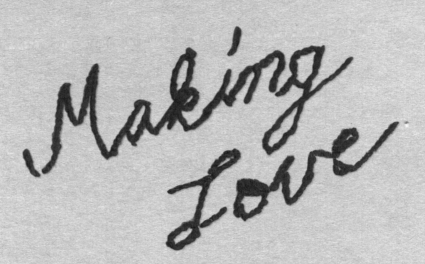

A wise marriage counselor once said, "A romantic relationship is like painting a bridge. The partners start at opposite ends of the span and paint toward the middle, and if one of the partners sets the brush down and stops painting, the bridge is going to rust." The lesson could not be clearer: craft inside.

Whether it is turning pinecones into back-scratchers, a sock into a monkey, or painting a lamp shade constructed from Popsicle sticks, crafting brings lovers together, and helps them stay together. The key is to let go in the craft room. Allow those inhibitions to float away. Once you do, you will find that working together, whether adding rickrack to pot holders or gluing eyes to coconuts, can be every bit as sensuous as helping your lover to an orgasm. That is because both crafting and lovemaking are about sharing. In the bedroom, you discover all sorts of secrets about your lover's body: the most pleasing way to stimulate their genitals, what bits to stroke and when. Does probing the anus feel natural, or is that just strange? Crafting is much the same. Crafting with a lover is a give-and-take—who cuts the felt, who applies the macaroni—and it is this give-and-take that can be so arousing.

Another beautiful part of creating a project together is that lovers get to experience the joy of nurturing something they care for, without the downside of repeatedly having to bail it out of jail. When a couple fails at crafting, they can simply toss the project away, gather up new construction paper and a handful of fresh glitter, uncap the rubber cement, and start afresh. Failing outside of the craft room means having to answer a lot of annoying questions from nosy neighbors, such as, "Was that your son Barry I saw on the news up in that clock tower with the rifle?"

Fornicrafting

Of all the crafts lovers can do together—woodworking, felt construction, googly eye application—making love can be the most enjoyable. The craft of lovemaking is simple to initiate, yet difficult to accomplish. Even for the amateur crafter, the starting point is obvious: roll up the sleeves, take aim, and begin poking about the pubicly-tufted fleshy parts. But without instruction, this random rummaging seldom leads to a gratifying experience. Careful consideration, preparation, and execution are a must for a joyful fornicrafting experience.

Disappointments in the bedroom can lead to a mouthful.

Beautifying the Pleasure Patch

No crafter in his right mind would start a project with a messy craft bench. Without an organized workspace, a minor sequin emergency can become a nerve-racking nightmare. So, imagine sitting down to your project table and finding it overgrown, matted, and infested with pests. This is not the environment that would be conducive to spraying a Styrofoam ball with glue and then covering it with jingles. That is why it is important to keep the pelvic hedge neat and trim. But never completely denude the frolic plot, because nature's shrubbery is there for a reason: it reduces external friction during intercourse and acts as a visual indicator for the thrill bits. Feel free to get creative with your groin-scaping; often it can act as a statement about one's personal style.

Familiarize Yourself with the Cavorting Implements

Most projects, in order to be successful, require the right tool for the job. But not only is the right tool important, a working knowledge of the device is also a must. Do your homework. Learn about the vast array of apparatuses on the market and what they do. Choose a few that interest you and bring them home. Seal yourself up in the craft room, disrobe, and let the sparks fly. Probe areas of your body that have long been designated for other purposes by nature and most state governments. Take notes. Once you feel you have found the implements that suit you and you feel confident using them, corner your partner and, applying the tool of your choice, prod and poke your lover with the type of gusto that would make even the most seasoned masseuse swoon.

Cleanup

Make no bones about it, the craft of lovemaking is a messy business, but this unfortunate fact shouldn't keep you from the craft of making love. In order to hasten cleanup time afterward it is important to prepare your environment before things get out of hand. Protect your lovemaking surface. The first thing that comes to most people's minds for a protective covering is newspaper, and while it's clearly better than nothing, fluids will still soak through onto your bedding, dining room table, leather car seats, etc. An ideal covering is an old shower curtain. Instead of tossing your mildew-encrusted plastic shower curtains away, scrub them down, dry them off, fold them, and store them away for the next time you and your partner are feeling frolicsome.

• • •

Now that you have prepared yourself to engage in the act of carnalizing your lover or lovers, you are ready to delve into the next section, a step-by-step guide to help you realize a fully penetrating coital transaction.

Beautifying the Pleasure Patch

Fellas

SERGEANT YORK
Closely shorn with a low fade on either side of the acorn.

THE DUST BOWL
Cut into a circular plot, seemingly unkempt, but purposely scruffy.

THE TOREADOR
Short crop in the center with bulbous protuberances of oval thickets on each side resembling pelt-like ears.

GOPHER'S NEST
Tightly coiled spiral-type curl, tapered up, collecting in a tidy mound. A small margin is cut around the "rodent" hole leaving ample clearance for the "gopher" to "pop his head out."

Ladies

THE SIZZLE STRIP
Hair sharply removed from the sides to form a long, centered, vertical rectangle.

STALIN'S MUSTACHE
A shorter yet bushier version of "The Sizzle Strip."

THE BOLL WEEVIL
A woolly middle patch accented by multiple flyaway tentacles.

THE MUTTONCHOP
Narrow on the top end and widening toward the bottom.

THE OLE GRANDDAD
Bristly in the center, bookended by wispy flourishes.

Smells

Touching

Touching can be an incredibly erotic prelude to intercourse. Too often, our inclination is to go stampeding for the genitals. We don't take the time to explore our lover's additional erogenous sectors through considerate stroking. Although it contradicts most of our romantic instincts, sometimes a casual fondle can be more sensuous then a sturdy poke, a delicate pet more arousing than a firm jab. Yes, there are plenty of times during lovemaking where manhandling the flapjacks, or harshly clawing at the acorn pouch is the most seductive course of action, but don't forget that occasionally, nothing gets the frolic juice flowing quite like a tender caress.

Smells

Lovemaking involves close physical contact. Don't be startled by peculiar aromas. Even though this curious musk can be a real eye opener, it is completely wholesome. Disagreeable bodily secretions are a natural part of us, but if you find this unusual gamey bouquet unpalatable, you can mask the environment using scented oils or a candle. Be brave, and savor the musk.

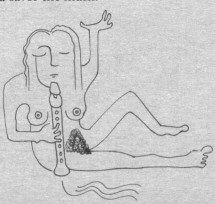

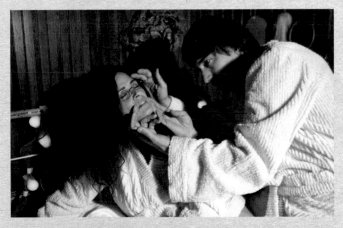

Massage

Nothing is a better prelude to sex than the act of rigorous kneading and merciless manhandling of the various body parts. Massage is a wonderful way to explore sensuality and an even better way to test your abilities of persuasion, for massage is definitely a case where it is better to receive than to give. Before digging in, it's a good idea to set the mood by dimming the lights, playing soft music, lighting a candle, and sprucing up the area with a festive selection of throw pillows. Warm your hands and make sure your nails have been clipped and filed. Nobody wants to be rubbed by a badger except another badger. Applying aromatic oils to the skin helps significantly reduce chafing. It's helpful to have a strategy mapping out your point of attack. It's never a bad plan to storm the area in and around the neck by digging your fingers into the shoulder blades. From there, sweep down the spine, occasionally pausing for minor skirmishes in the lower back region and along the buttocks. Continue to march south through the back of the thighs and calves, saving the feet for the final conflict. A massage is a wonderful start to further erotic adventures!

Dried bean pods make wonderful exotic instruments in the bedroom.

Fantasize

Feet

One of the most overlooked pleasure zones are the feet. This could be due to the fact that they are located all the way at the bottom of the leg, but more likely has to do with the way they appear after walking through the streets in sandals. Applying erratic pressure to your lover's instep not only titillates, but it helps build trust by demonstrating that you are willing to touch their feet. Not only are the hoofs a way to receive amusement, they can also deliver. Sure it's easy to imagine punting a soccer ball or changing the station on a car radio with your feet, but did you know that a rough callus on the big toe, when applied to your partner's clitoris, can be an incredible stimulating implement?

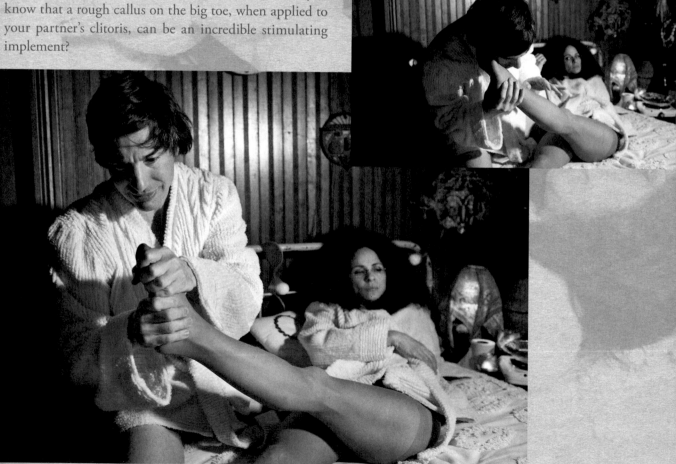

Sexual Missteps

A healthy sexual encounter can be a frenzied affair, an unrestrained flurry of senseless depravity. In the moment, gripped by a chaotic orgiastic euphoria, it's easy to cross the line of good judgment. This includes playing too rough, screaming out past lovers' names, or attempting to lodge an appendage or toy in an orifice where you have not been thoroughly invited. If entering the wrong hole does occur, and your partner becomes upset, it is important to appear sensitive to their feelings. Put your own desires on hold, understanding that if the situation doesn't quickly resolve, you can always finish your needs on your own time. For now, patience is the key, and the best thing you can do is to hold your partner tight and make a face that suggests you are listening.

Rusty nails make terrific love chimes.

Cuddle Time

For most men, once they've orgasmed, it's time to move on to television or computer games, unless another orgasm is involved. But most men haven't seen two orgasms since the days they had a paper route. For women, cuddling is an essential part of lovemaking. The act of cuddling releases a hormone called "oxytocin," that provokes a feeling known as "pair bonding." Post-orgasm, men release a hormone as well, called "mucho siesta," provoking a feeling of nappy.

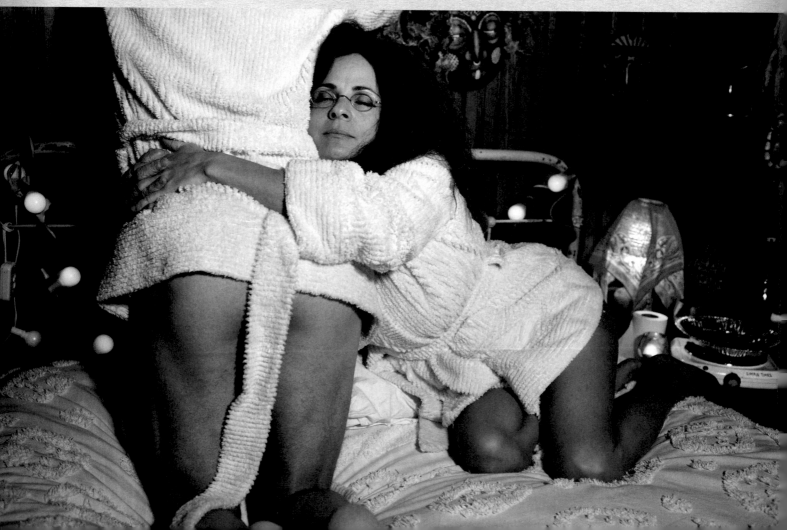

Tickle Rod

If you are feeling it's time to spice up your love life, but not sure how to talk your lover into allowing sex toys to take over some of the monotonous duties that you're having trouble mounting enthusiasm for, the following steps might prove helpful. Sex toys, like all tools, allow us to be more efficient with less effort. When introducing sex toys into your sex play, be careful that your lover does not view the merrymaking implement as simply a way for you to shirk responsibility but rather as a playful friend who has come to lend a helping hand. When introducing any sex toy, make sure to spring it on your partner. Surprise may be your only ally. The last thing to keep in mind, once you have successfully introduced your lover to a sex toy, is to make your application of that implement seem difficult. Mimic the faces of rock guitarists when they play a solo. This will keep your lover in the mood, by fooling them into believing you are engaged, and not thinking about the dead tree you have to cut down and drag to the curb before it falls on the carport.

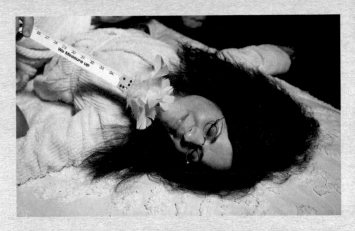

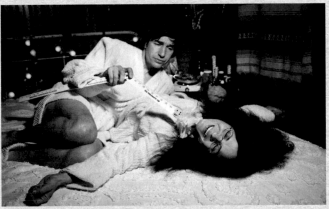

Responsible for Your Own Orgasm

An orgasm is much like the final available seat on the last lifeboat of a sinking ocean liner: everybody for themselves! Don't expect an orgasm to be handed to you like a free cup of coffee. You must be aggressive in your pursuit, not unlike a raccoon foraging in a trash can for any edible morsel. Having an orgasm is not a race, but still it's important to win. Have you ever seen a track event? Take sprinters, for instance. The first racer across the line gets all the attention. The winning runner is celebrated and focused on. Nobody is paying attention to the second-place finisher. When a couple is having sex, after the first orgasm occurs, you can pretty much count on 50% of the enthusiasm leaving the room.

Happy Endings

So, it is clear crafting and lovers go together like tuna and melt. Whether crafting together in a craft room, or fornicrafting in the bedroom, both are activities that couples can share, bringing lovers together. Making love will leave a couple with wonderful memories, and crafting will leave a couple with special items that were created together and unfortunately will be viciously argued over when that same couple splits up, each cursing the other while they go their separate ways.

AVOCADO NIGHT CREAM

Materials:

4 tablespoons beeswax

2 tablespoons cocoa butter

5 tablespoons avocado oil

1 tablespoon olive oil

¼ teaspoon borax

4 tablespoons rosewater

Instructions: Melt beeswax over low heat in the top of a double boiler. When beeswax has melted, add cocoa butter and avocado oil. Stir well. Add the olive oil, blend. Dissolve the borax in the rosewater and add to the mixture. Remove from heat. Continue to stir until cream has thickened and cooled. Store night cream in a cool place. Will keep for 2 months.

Courtesy of Antonia Xereas.

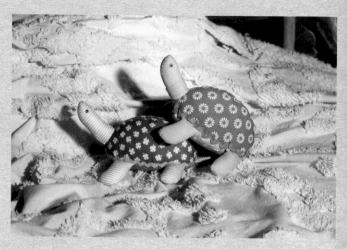

Keep things slow and easy.

SMELLY OIL

For stinky times.

Instructions: Fill a tinfoil pie pan with some water and add an essential oil. Place the pan on a hot plate and leave it by the side of your bed. This aroma will enhance the lovemaking mood.

Courtesy of Callie Thorne.

CORKSCREW CANDLES

Instructions: Take two pieces of corkscrew trim about five inches in length. Glue the two flat sides together, creating a candle shape. Dribble with hot glue to create the appearance of melted wax, and paint white.

BROWN SUGAR AND LAVENDER BODY SCRUB

White sugar

Brown sugar

4 drops lavender oil

2 drops mineral oil

Baby oil

Instructions: Place the white and brown sugar in a container first. Add the lavender oil, then mix. Add mineral oil. Add baby oil until the mixture has a paste-like consistency.

Courtesy of Shannon Thompson.

PANTY HOSE LIGHTS

Instructions: Run a string of lights through the leg of a pair of panty hose. Attach a twist tie between the lights. To make the twist ties, cut a piece of wire and sandwich between 2 pieces of colorful tape. Run lights along your bed's headboard.

MEASURE THE PLEASURE TICKLE ROD

Instructions: Attach a wad of colorful lightweight feathers to the end of a yardstick or ruler. Tickle your partner and watch them "let go."

EDUCATIONAL CLOCK

The bedroom is for enticing. You don't want to think about the time in there, so I recommend making a fake clock.

Instructions: Not included in this book.

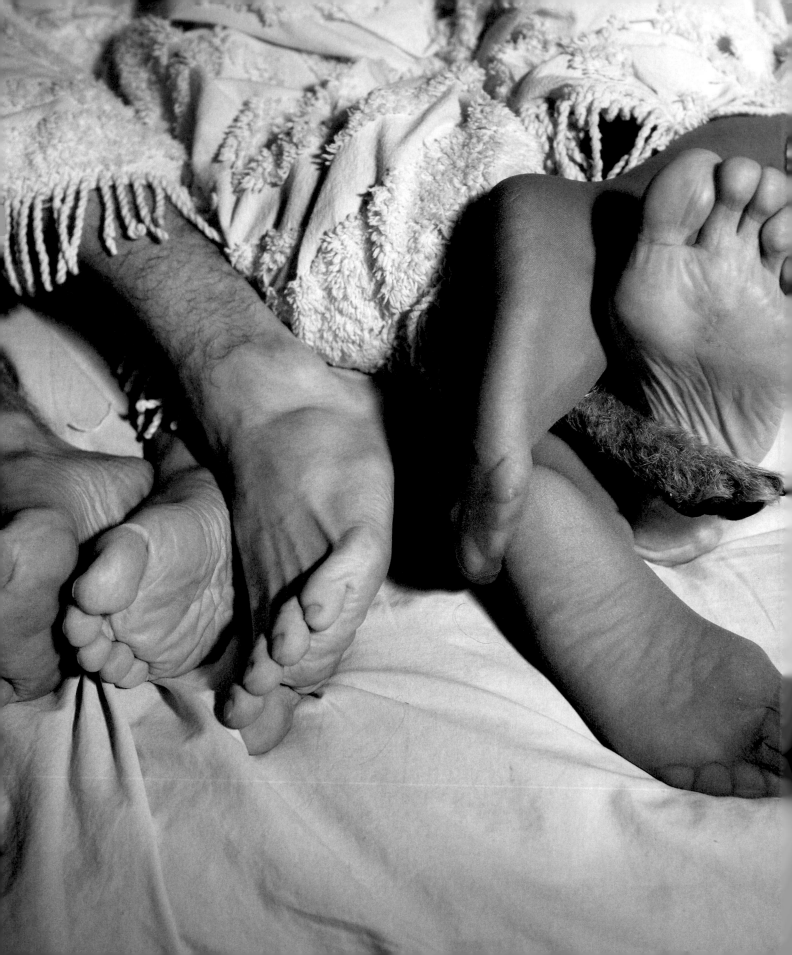

Jean and Gene Woodchuck: "A Special Corner"

Let's make no bones about it, we are a highly sexual couple. We don't have what some would say is a perfect marriage and we'll be the first to admit it. Sure, our sacred union is missing a few nuts and bolts. For example, we don't have a strong line of communication, can't say we trust each other, and we certainly don't have what you might call a mutual respect, but get a few drinks in us, and we make up for whatever might be lacking with some prime choice U.S. grade-A humping. Except, here's the twist, we're not talking about humping each other, know what we mean? You see, in order for us to keep things spicy, we have an open marriage, wide open; the swinging door has come off the hinges. What we found is that the best way for us to share is by sharing ourselves with strangers. We do that by hosting weekly groping jamborees at our place. Let's us take you through a night of mob passion. First off, we lock up the dogs. We've tried to let them roam free in the past, but trust us, naked sweaty bodies mixed with warm dog fur is an unpleasant combination. Next, we cover anything that can be soiled by fluids in vinyl tarps. We'd advise you to think broadly here. Sure some things are obvious to semen-proof, like the mattresses and the couch, but trust us, we've found fun batter in some pretty strange places: inside the refrigerator, dribbled over our incomplete set of encyclopedias, and there was a hanging fern that had to be vigorously hosed down. So be liberal with the plastic. It is also nice to present your guests with snacks. We're big on the chips and salsa. It's easy to prepare and it seems to be a good prelude to what we are always hoping will be an unforgettable evening of zesty fumbling. You might be wondering how to go about finding people to participate. It's easier than you think. We advertise in a couple of magazines, word of mouth helps, and you'd be surprised how many people we meet on buses that are all too happy to come on over to our place, have a few snacks, and scrabble about in the nude.

So, the bottom line is this—if you feel like your love life has stalled, open it up to any and all takers. Let the warm juices fly! Swinging fixed our relationship. Well, at least made it tolerable.

SAUSAGES

Mexicans call it chorizo, Bob Evans calls them links.
The Germans have a knackwurst, with all the beer they drink.
The Polish say "kielbasa!" when it's time to eat.
I just call them sausages, but I never call them meat.
—Gene Woodchuck

he first sausage was probably made out of the necessity to use all the parts of the animal: unidentifiable scraps of meat and organs, too tough to chew, seasoned and then stuffed into the intestines of that same animal. Curiously, they are made exactly the same way today.

Types of Sausage

There are many different types of sausages: fresh, dry, smoked, and blood to name a few. We will focus on fresh, since these are the easiest to make on the quick.

Meat

Any meat can be used to make sausage, but the key is to make sure you have enough fat. Some people actually choose to add more fat in the form of fatback (pork), chicken fat (poultry), or suet (beef). These culinary daredevils are the same people who smoke cigarettes to aid digestion, and snack on "corn nuts."

Salt!

Salt not only acts as a preservative in sausage, it is also the flavor. All sausages have to have salt. Including the meat, the salt is probably the most important ingredient, although the fat gives the salt a pretty good run for its money. The amount you use in each recipe depends on personal taste and the mysteriousness of the "meat" used. Fresh sausages have less salt than dry. Dry sausage needs extra salt to ward off harmful bacteria. One might believe that this information would ward off most people from eating dry sausage.

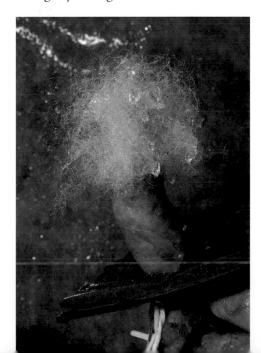

Flavorings/Additions

This is where you can get creative. Whatever type of sausage you make, try to remember that you don't want to kill the flavor of the meat you are using. Some sausages will simply use salt and pepper, while others use herbs and spices. You might want to start out simple, adding fennel seeds or white wine and hot pepper flakes.

Some sausages have other additions like raisins, dried cranberries, nuts, jalapeños, or pieces of truffles. You can put in anything you want, considering that the bar has already been shattered by the quality of meat used in the first place.

Casings

There are a few choices when it comes to casings. The most common are pig, which are fairly large (think Italian sausage) and sheep, which are thinner (think hot dogs). "Casings" is a polite way to say "pig and sheep intestines that have been cleaned and preserved with salt." This reminds me of an old butcher joke: A proper woman walks into a butcher shop and inquires about the sausages. The butcher behind the counter explains that the casings are the intestines of a pig. The lady, shocked, explains her hesitancy about eating meat stuffed into a pig intestine, considering what used to come out of it, and the butcher says, "Lady, you wouldn't worry about what came out of it, if you had any idea what I shoved into it!"

When working with these natural casings you need to rinse them thoroughly as if what passed through them actually passed through them, which it did. Make sure you squeeze them as dry as possible. Before you stuff your sausages you will need to tie off one end of the casing and thread it onto the funnel of your sausage stuffer. You need to take care when doing this because the casing can rip. Which reminds me of another butcher joke. How did the butcher catch gonorrhea while working? The casing on his sausage ripped!

There are also man-made casings made of collagen (flavorless meat paper), which are completely edible and easy to use, but leave a papery skin on the sausage whereas the natural casing lends a nice snap. This meat paper is also good to use for homework that can actually be eaten by a dog.

Grinding

When grinding meat for sausage you can use many different types of contraptions. The old grinder your grandmother might have used with the hand crank is still a great low-cost option.

The key to grinding your meat is to have all of your ingredients and equipment as cold as possible. (Note: Oddly, no butcher jokes exist concerning the topic of "grinding your meat.") When grinding, the pieces of meat should fit through the hole of the grinder, so before you season them you will have to cut them into about one-inch cubes. A good tip is to grind your sausages at least two times, chilling the meat between grindings. This gives the finished sausage a finer texture.

Stuffing

There are a few ways you can get the sausage into the casings. You can do it by hand with a funnel, which is very time consuming and gets boring fast. The second way is by using the grinder on your stand mixer with a funnel attachment. This works well and probably is the most accessible to home cooks. The third way is to use the plunger-type stuffer to stuff your meat, which most smaller-scale professionals use and, if you're keeping score, is the most double-entendre-like.

SWEET ITALIAN

Good basic Italian sausage, best when cooked on the day you make it.

SERVES 6

2 pounds pork butt (cut into 1-inch cubes)

¼ cup white wine

¼ teaspoon black pepper

1 tablespoon salt

¼ teaspoon fennel seeds

⅛ teaspoon grated orange rind

¼ teaspoon red pepper flakes

3 to 4 feet hog casing

Mix all of the ingredients together, except for the casings, and refrigerate overnight. Grind two times, first through a large grinding plate and then chill your meat for a half hour. Then grind through the fine plate. Set up your grinder with the sausage funnel attachment. Tie one end of the cleaned casing and thread it onto the funnel. Slowly push your ground meat mixture through the grinder and fill until the casings feel firm. Leave a little slack at the end of the casings then twist the sausage into links. Tie the end and let sit for a half hour before cooking.

Courtesy of Frank Proto.

BREAKFAST PATTIES

These are hand-formed—no need for casings—and are quick to make.

SERVES 6

2 pounds ground pork

4 ounces ground fatback

2 teaspoons salt

1 teaspoon ground black pepper

1 tablespoon brown sugar

¼ teaspoon dry sage

1 pinch ground cloves

⅛ teaspoon red pepper flakes

Mix all of the ingredients together. Form into patties and cook until browned.

Courtesy of Frank Proto.

CHORIZO

Spicy Mexican-style.

SERVES 6

2 pounds pork butt

6 ounces fatback

2 tablespoons smoked paprika

1 tablespoon chili flakes

⅛ teaspoon cumin

1 chipotle, minced

1 white onion, diced

2 cloves garlic, minced

1½ tablespoons salt

1 teaspoon black pepper

3 to 4 feet hog casing

(Same directions as Sweet Italian sausage only with a spicy flair.)

Courtesy of Frank Proto.

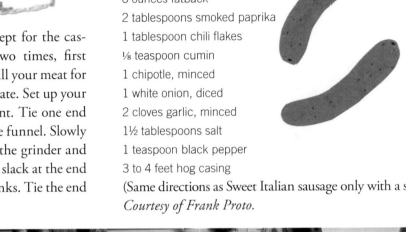

SMOKY SAUSAGE LINK SMOKE HOUSE (SEE PAGE 256)
Instructions: Pan-fry your link sausages until golden brown, saving the grease drippings from the pan to pour over smoke house when you are done. Build your smoke house by attaching the pan-fried links together using toothpicks. Make the roof out of corrugated cardboard. To create the puffin' smoke stack, make a finger-sized hole in the roof, and stuff a link sausage in the top and apply cotton batting.

TAR HEEL SAUSAGE COOKIES

The only reason I wanted to include a section in the book about sausages is that I have wanted to make a hairdo out of sausages for years. My knowledge of sausage was solely culled from attending a wedding once in the mountains at which sausage cookies were served. I ate too many and got sick to my stomach. I'm guessing on the recipe here but I suggest you make a chocolate chip cookie dough by following the back of a chocolate chip morsel bag and substitute sausage for the chips. You probably don't have to grease the cookie sheet.

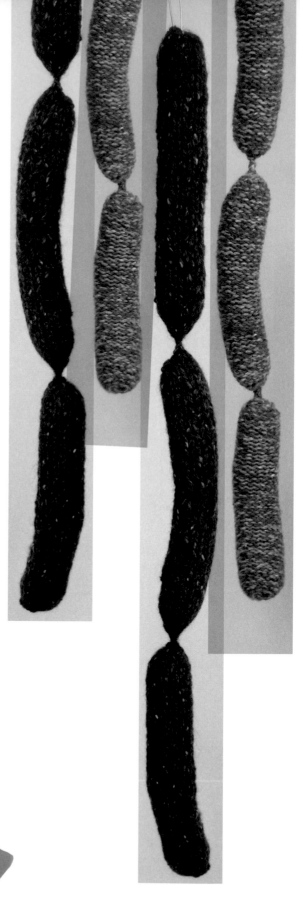

Pickles!

take
time out
for a
hobby

KNOWING YOUR KNACK FOR KNICKKNACKS

Home Furnishings

Whether you live in an igloo, a boathouse, or a camper, your home furnishings, or more specifically, trivial ornament arrangements, are an expression of who you are. Each room tells a story about you. It may be a short story, a comedy, or even a tragedy. But because this story is so personal, it is best told by a stranger—namely, an interior decorator. These people are professionals, and although they won't have the first clue about how to capture what is unique about you, they are adept at organizing your clutter effectively enough so that when people visit, you can fool them into believing you are not completely unhinged. The major drawback to interior designers is not that they are traditionally homosexual, but that they can be very expensive. This unfortunately leaves most of us to tell our own stories. In order to avoid having your story turn out to be one that kills the party, here are a few tips to follow when accentuating your space with crafty bits of you.

Assessing Your Abode

Before you can tell your story, you need to understand your space. Don't concern yourself with such insignificant elements as size, shape, or building style, but simply focus on what is missing from the space. Harshly judge your area the same way you would a blind date. Does the space lack attractiveness? Is it dull or accessorized in a cheap fashion? Is it the wrong color? Too Oriental? Is that thinning, or is the light just hitting the head funny? Once you have made this assessment, simply fill the space with what it is lacking or pretend to use the restroom, hail a cab, and never look back, depending on what exactly we are talking about.

Symmetry

Symmetry is important. This means having the same presentation of items on both sides of an imagined or real centerline. It is crucial to balance every one-of-a-kind object with another one exactly like it. When crafting for yourself, it is a good idea to craft in twos. Pairs are generally more pleasing. We can all relate to the awkwardness of having one kidney or an only child. Don't put yourself in an embarrassing situation of having to explain why your mantel appears to list to one side, weighted by only one pinch pot.

Rhythm

Rhythm is another vital element to home furnishings. Or, in other words, do da doodads flow? Rhythm is characterized by creating a pattern and then repeating it. As discussed earlier, pairs are pleasing, so now imagine the infinite joy of hundreds of toilet paper roll pirates stretched around the room, creating an endless loop of tiny cardboard swashbucklers! Talk about style! When positioning your handcrafted doohickeys about the room, be careful that one thingamabob leads pleasantly into the next whatchamacallit. For example, does it make sense to place, upon a mantel, miniature wooden shoes next to a terra-cotta snail? Let's find out. Little shoes make us think of small feet, which makes us think of midgets, which leads us to the circus and then to peanuts, which leads to elephants, causing us to think of ivory, then piano keys, which are white and black, then of course the Ku Klux Klan, which makes us think of adorable hoods, from which we think of Red Riding Hood, then a wolf dressed like Grandma, reminding us of transvestites, which makes us think of hirsute dancing girls, then of course, the French cabaret, the French love to eat escargot, terra-cotta snails! Yes, it makes perfect sense.

Tassels!

Tassels are facile and never a hassle
Hung from your curtains home is a castle
Flawlessly fluffed tufts of loose-flowing thread
Carefree on one end, knotted at the head.
A lovely metaphor for the way to live life
Simultaneously secure, while casually blithe.

So, for the perfect adornment, tassels I suggest!
Tie back a drape with style and zest.
Dangle from a mortarboard or twirl from
your breast
Like a sultan affix them to shoes and a vest
For a frill or a trimming, tassels are best.

—Gene Woodchuck

...tive Fridays!

Nature's Way

AT REST

Knowing Your Knack for KNICKKNACKS

SHUT-INS

The Joy of Poverty

PEP TALK

...ssAGES

Creative

Unreturnable Gift Giving

Out of this world

costumes

...tive Fridays

COCONUTS!

Making Love ♥

Handicraftable

Teenagers Have ALOT OF PAIN

Fireside Story telling

Crafting for Jesus

CRAFTY CANDLESTICKS!

Fridays

CONFECTIONERIES

Safety Meeting

Simple Times

Creative Fr

HAY BURNERS

Craft yourself Homely

Nothing lends itself to clubs quite like crafting. It's getting together weekly with like-minded people who offer support and encouragement, not unlike Alcoholics Anonymous, but with a craft club, the "hitting rock bottom" stories are far more harrowing. Another small difference is alcohol. All the best craft clubs are fueled by drugs and alcohol—how else can one stay amused while rhinestoning? At my craft club, Creative Fridays, we always recite this verse before each meeting:

Dear Lord,
Please give us the strength to accept
the things we have made. The courage to not
take credit for what we have not—
And the wisdom to know the difference.
My name is [Blank], and I am a crafter.

As mentioned in "Safety Meeting," murder is one downside of belonging to a craft club, but there are also plenty of benefits. Clubs are proven motivators. You will find that you will accomplish much more when crafting within a club circle than on your own, and the key factor is judgment. This is the same way Fat Busters makes people lose weight: members expressing shallow opinions about you. Guess what? It should be a little easier to avoid going home after a meeting and eating a whole pound cake after your major supporter has sensitively expressed his opinion of your current state by saying, "Jesus H. Christ, your scale at home must work in reverse, because I swear to all that's holy, it looks like your torso is trying to swallow your head." In the same way, no one will judge your crafting abilities more helpfully harshly than your own craft circle. That is because the secret to empowerment is feeling superior to the people around you, so you can bet the constructive criticism is going to fly. I find it is always a good idea to invite at least one person who clearly has no artistic ability into your craft club. That way everybody can collectively judge this person and feel much better about the whatever it is they are crafting.

I also have found all successful craft clubs need a strict set of rules to follow. I keep one copy of these posted in the craft room, and another posted next to the toilet.

CRAFT LAWS

1. YOU BREAKY YOU BOUGHTY!

This is a general house rule. Crafting can become a raucous affair: I've been shut down by the law on more than one occasion. The point is, I can't keep my eye on every piece of property I own, so I've enacted this simple policy. You destroy something in my house, you get me a new one, no questions asked, other than, "When am I getting my new one?" Now some have made the ridiculous accusation that I'm taking advantage of this home law by purposely placing worn-out luxury items in precarious places in order to have them replaced with new ones I don't have to pay for, which I find insulting. Is it really that strange to balance a television on the edge of a sink?

2. NO HETEROSEXUAL COUPLES!

I always say, "If you are going to bring a lover to my crafting circle, you better bring enough for everybody." Nobody who is attempting to drown their loneliness in a decoupage project wants to look up and see two crafters nuzzling. Although, I do give homosexuals a break on this policy, because when it comes to crafting, it pays to keep them happy.

3. NO SPECIAL DIETARY NEEDS

No one will suck the energy out of a crafting circle quicker than a vegan. Part of the beauty of a craft club is the opportunity to indulge any whim you might have, and if that includes a tub of ice cream, so be it.

4. YOU SMOKE IT OR DRINK IT, YOU BRING IT

I will be the first to admit that I like to be completely plied with drugs and alcohol before I'll even pick up a pixie stick or a hot glue gun. I couldn't imagine crafting without being on the verge of hallucination, but my days of supplying drugs to anyone who wanted them ended in grade school, and I don't mean when I went to grade school, but rather sold drugs to grade-schoolers.

5. NO TWO PEOPLE TAKING BREAKS AT THE SAME TIME

When you craft in my club you're here to work, and you're here to work for me. I set the agenda and I want to see results. For instance, sometimes the craft for the evening might be a painting project, specifically painting my hallway, or a night of "bookcase building" crafting. So there is no time for relaxing—besides I'm always on break. So when you craft at my place, the break room is sold out, should have booked ahead, no exceptions, *capisce*? Another reason I don't allow breaks, especially two crafters to break at the same time, is that this allows them to talk when they are not in my presence and that's how dissension starts. Next thing you know they are staging a craft coup.

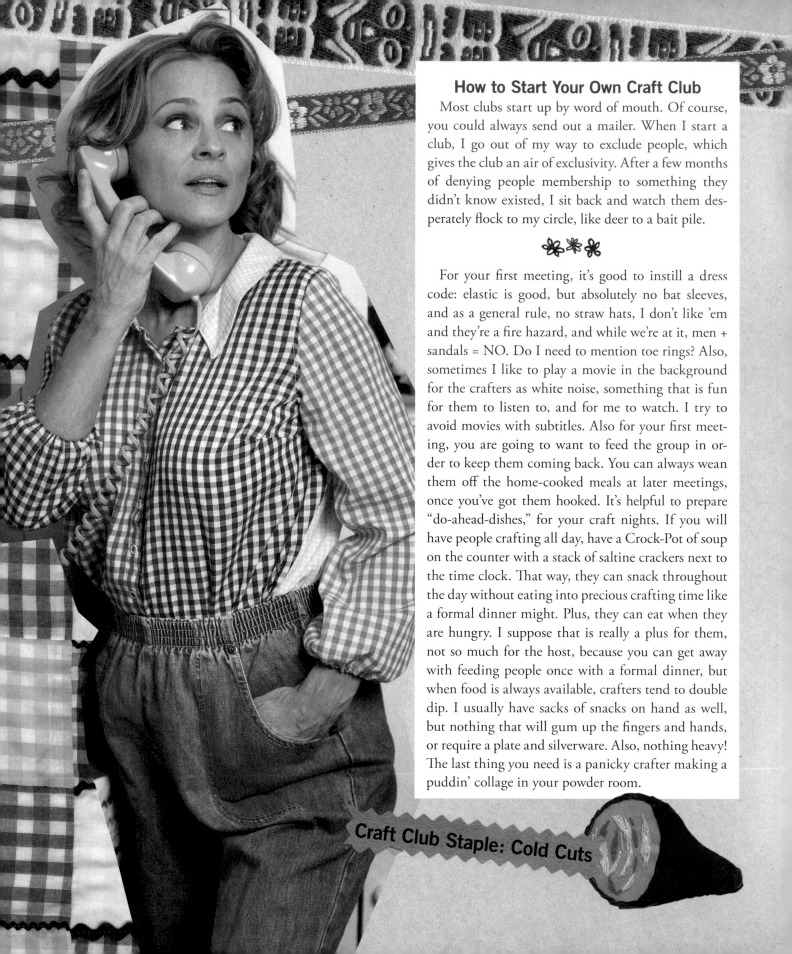

How to Start Your Own Craft Club

Most clubs start up by word of mouth. Of course, you could always send out a mailer. When I start a club, I go out of my way to exclude people, which gives the club an air of exclusivity. After a few months of denying people membership to something they didn't know existed, I sit back and watch them desperately flock to my circle, like deer to a bait pile.

❀✳❀

For your first meeting, it's good to instill a dress code: elastic is good, but absolutely no bat sleeves, and as a general rule, no straw hats, I don't like 'em and they're a fire hazard, and while we're at it, men + sandals = NO. Do I need to mention toe rings? Also, sometimes I like to play a movie in the background for the crafters as white noise, something that is fun for them to listen to, and for me to watch. I try to avoid movies with subtitles. Also for your first meeting, you are going to want to feed the group in order to keep them coming back. You can always wean them off the home-cooked meals at later meetings, once you've got them hooked. It's helpful to prepare "do-ahead-dishes," for your craft nights. If you will have people crafting all day, have a Crock-Pot of soup on the counter with a stack of saltine crackers next to the time clock. That way, they can snack throughout the day without eating into precious crafting time like a formal dinner might. Plus, they can eat when they are hungry. I suppose that is really a plus for them, not so much for the host, because you can get away with feeding people once with a formal dinner, but when food is always available, crafters tend to double dip. I usually have sacks of snacks on hand as well, but nothing that will gum up the fingers and hands, or require a plate and silverware. Also, nothing heavy! The last thing you need is a panicky crafter making a puddin' collage in your powder room.

Craft Club Staple: Cold Cuts

CROCK-POT COUNTRY KITCHEN BARBECUED RIBS

- 1 18 OUNCE BOTTLE OF YOUR FAVORITE BBQ SAUCE
- 3 POUNDS COUNTRY STYLE CUT RIBS IN SERVING-SIZE PORTIONS
- ADD A LITTLE SAUCE TO THE BOTTOM OF YOUR CROCK POT
- ADD THE RIBS AND THE REST OF THE SAUCE
- COVER AND COOK FOR 9 HOURS!

COURTESY OF ANNE VIGLIAROLO.

Ideas

MORE
FUN
CRAFTS
THIS WAY
→

CROCK-POT BEEF AND VEGETABLES

1 POUND POTATOES CUT INTO FOURTHS
1 CUP OF CHOPPED CARROTS
3 TABLESPOON DIJON MUSTARD
SALT AND PEPPER, TO TASTE
1 TEASPOON THYME, FRESHLY CHOPPED
2 TABLESPOON ROSEMARY, FRESHLY CHOPPED
3 POUNDS OF BONELESS BEEF CHUCK ROAST, TRIMMED OF FAT
1 SMALL ONION, FINELY CHOPPED
1½ CUP OF BEEF BROTH

- PLACE THE POTATOES AND CARROTS IN CROCK-POT
- MIX THE MUSTARD, SALT AND PEPPER, THYME, AND ROSEMARY. SPREAD THE MIXTURE OVER THE BEEF AND PUT IT IN CROCK-POT. TOP THE BEEF WITH THE ONIONS AND POUR BROTH OVER EVERYTHING.
- COVER AND COOK ON LOW HEAT FOR 9½ HOURS!

COURTESY OF ANNE VIGLIAROLO.

CROCK-POT SQUASH

2 MEDIUM ACORN SQUASH
1 16 OUNCE CAN WHOLE CRANBERRY SAUCE
⅓ CUP ORANGE MARMALADE
¾ CUP RAISINS
1 TEASPOON QUICK-COOKING TAPIOCA
¼ TEASPOON CINNAMON

- REMOVE THE SEEDS FROM THE ACORN SQUASH
- CUT ONE SQUASH INTO 1-INCH RINGS AND THE SECOND SQUASH INTO A WEDGE, ARRANGE SQUASH IN CROCK-POT
- IN A BOWL, MIX THE CRANBERRY SAUCE, ORANGE MARMALADE, RAISINS, TAPIOCA, AND CINNAMON
- POUR MIXTURE OVER THE SQUASH
- COVER AND COOK ON A LOW HEAT FOR 4½ HOURS OR ON HIGH HEAT FOR 2½ HOURS!

RECIPE COURTESY OF ANNE VIGLIAROLO. SHE LOVES IT AND SO DOES EVERYONE ELSE!

Lace

Antiqued Deed

Cardboard Pizza Plates

Book Covers

Paint by Numbers

Mask

Stencils

Pot Holder

Papier Mâché

Miniature Paper Hat

Covered Lighter

Knitted Cap

Fingerpainting

Tissue Flowers

Big Hits

Easy $ell

Clown
Nose
-Red-

Hooks & Hinges

Eyeball
cut 2 Black
Blue eyes

TETANUS

PRISON
MOUSE

GENE'S CORNER

I don't like druggies. Me and Jean lead clean lives, which means if it don't come from nature, we don't put it down our gullet. That's why when we want to relax, we strictly go with grain alcohol, mushrooms, and of course God's herb, Mary Jane. Now, I used to think smoking grass was for pussies, until I discovered smoking it from out of a nut-and-bolt pipe. It's simple to make one, and this is how you do it: Unscrew a Cosgrove flout valve from the bottom of a Grinick joint. Put the flout valve in a Kromer vice with the hollow end up and drill with quarter-inch Bafley bit until the bit stops going down. Empty out the fillings from where there should now be a hole. Place the larger end of the Grinick joint into the vice, and using a no. 6 ⅝th horner spur point, make another hole. Now, using a hacksaw cut a two-inch section of pipe from Coaler boiler tubing. Screw the flout valve into the bottom of the Grinick joint, pushing the Coaler tubing onto the flamley stem of the Grinick joint where the check valve was. Now, TOKITY TOKE!

Nuts & Bolts

Support Your Local Artists

Salt Igloo

Ideas
→ →

Instructions: Make a salt igloo. Once that is finished, fold over a piece of construction paper in half. Cut into the shape of a flag. Open the flaps and add glue in the center and wrap it around a long toothpick. Place the flag between 2 fingers and use an up-and-down motion with your fingers to create the wave. Plant flag in igloo.

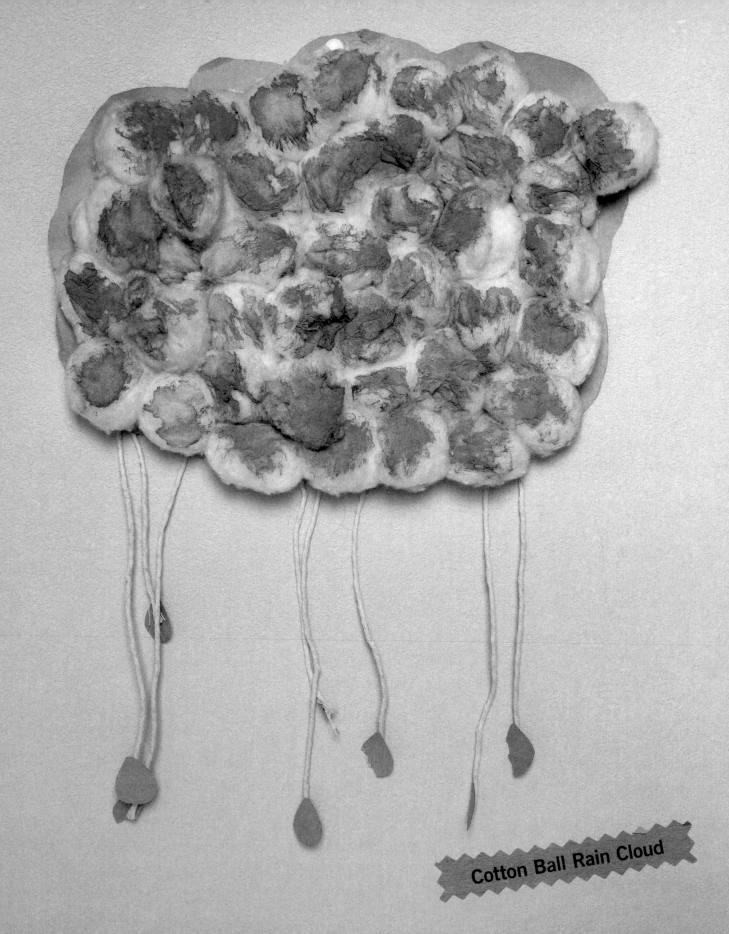

Cotton Ball Rain Cloud

Ideas → →

Tube Bong

Pompon Turn Around

Instructions: Apply an 18 x 18-inch pompon to an elastic band that is 9 inches wide. Scoot this over your toilet seat, with the seat closed so the pompon is sitting on top. When you need to use the toilet, flip the pompon around, lean back and enjoy the comfort. When finished simply remember to turn your pompon toilet seat cover back around; if you don't, it can get infested with urine, feces, toilet paper, and tampon applicators, as well as vomit and bacon grease.

Chest of Bonnets

Penny Splits-a-Lot

Knitting Holder Can

(AS SEEN ON COVER)
Instructions: Decorate the outside of an oatmeal canister. Make a hole in the center of the top. Drop your ball of yarn in the canister and run one end through the hole in the cover.

Tassel Belt

Seagull-Shaped Tape

Tongue Depressor Characters

Instructions: Eyeball it. For the "walk-on characters," place hair scraps in a jar, randomly apply glue to the tongue depressor ¼ inch down. Dip the stick in the hair, and wiggle it around a little. Pull out and work with that. These guys are big scene-stealers.

Steakhouse Fingernails

Instructions: You need circus peanuts for this craft and expect to go through a lot of them. Crack the peanuts open, remove the nut, find the right fit for the right fingertip. And slip it on. Draw the nails with Magic Marker. Label the inside of the shell so you know what finger and hand to put it back on. These look terrific with fingerless gloves.
Beware, nail-biters: these nails can cause pain when applying to finger; the shells will rub up against your sores causing more bleeding. Another option would be to apply skin-toned Band-Aids to your fingertips and paint the nails on top. Your nails will look real!

Miniature Witch Hat

Instructions: Cut a donut shape out of sturdy paper. Cover in black tape. Cut a half circle out of paper. Roll into a cone shape and tape in place. Cover this in black tape as well. Place cone shape inside the hole of the donut shape. You will see witch hat start to take shape. Snip excess bottom edge of cone to base of hat. Fold down edges and tape down.

Marching Sword

Instructions: Saw a 27-inch piece off one end of a yardstick. Make a point on the other end. With a hammer nail the other 9-inch piece that is left to the 27-inch piece, near the end. Paint the stick, which is now a sword, with enamel paint. Carry over shoulder. For children, you might want to just shadow your point onto the stick by drawing an outline of the point and coloring around it.

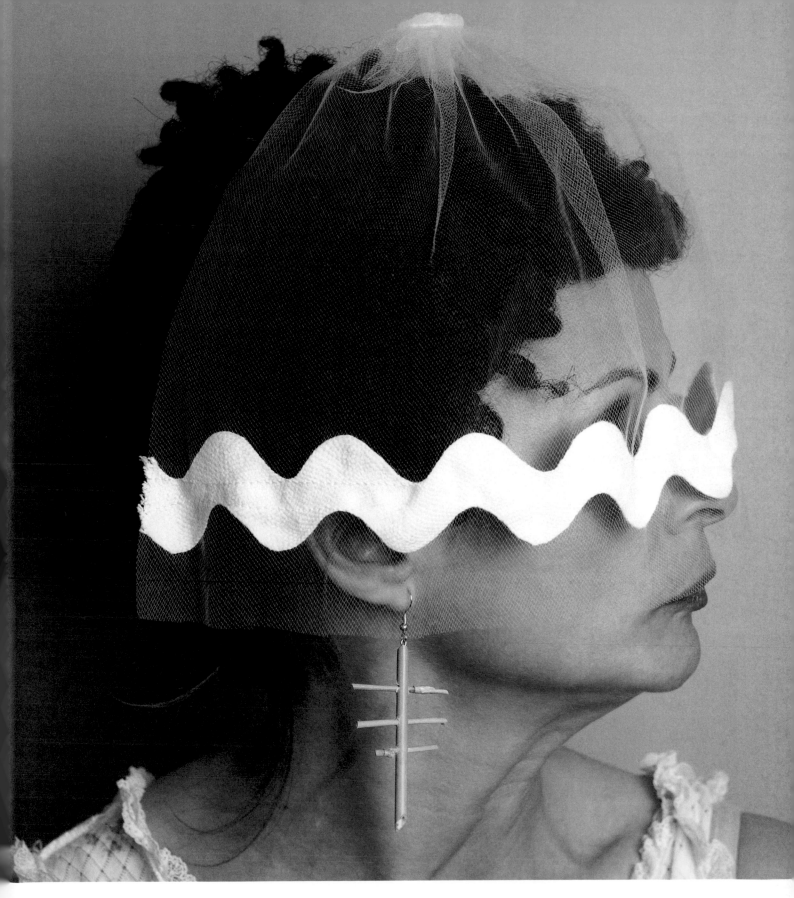

Clamshell Wedding Veils

Tools

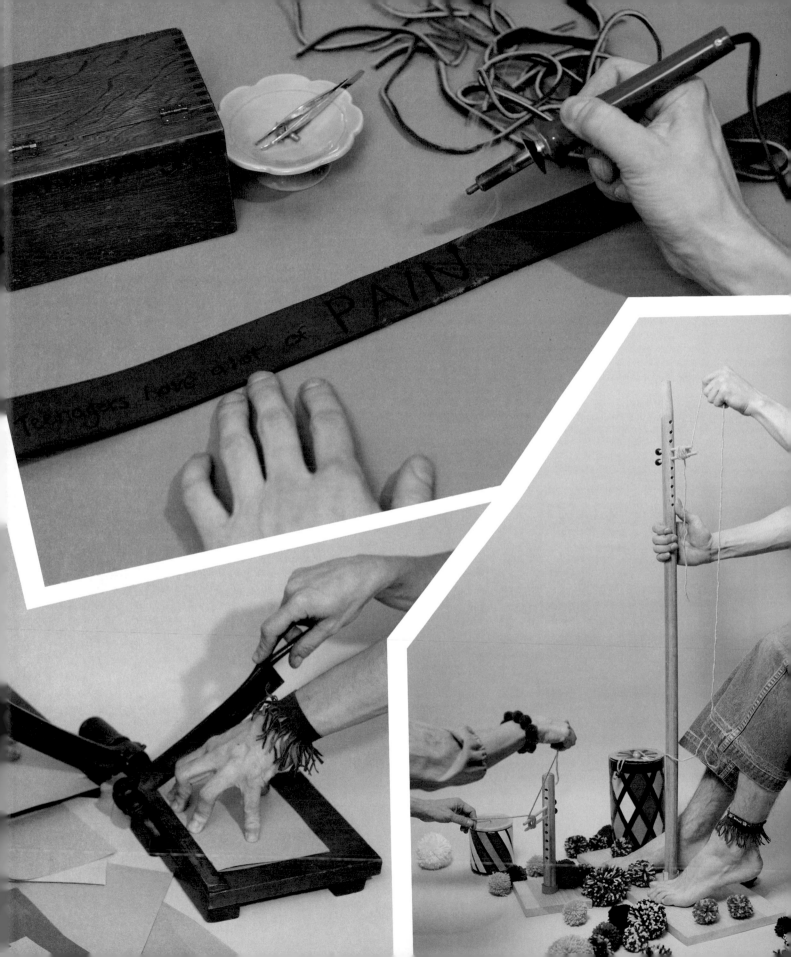

CRAFT ROOM NECESSITIES

Tissue paper	Beads	<u>Shavings</u>	
Colored chalk	Blocks of wood	Fake fingernails	
Rubber cement	Adhesive stars	Clamshells	
Paper punch	Fake fur	Spools	
<u>Wire</u>	<u>Colored tape</u>	<u>Sponges</u>	
Doilies	Toupee tape	<u>Tin cans</u>	
Washable ink	Rusty nails	Toilet tissue rolls	
Googly eyes	<u>Feathers</u>	Toothpicks	
Pipe cleaners	Cotton balls	Wood scraps	
Construction paper	Beans and seeds	Scissors, pinking	
Utility knife	Bottle caps	Shears	
Graveyard dirt	Pins	Glue	
Miniature shingles	Teeth	Masking tape	
<u>Elastic</u>	Burlap	Driftwood	
Bells	Buttons	Wood-burning kit	
Carpet scraps	Clothespins	Crepe paper	
<u>Box</u>	Corks	Matches	
Rickrack, trim	Drinking straws	Blow torch	
Cheesecloth	Egg cartons	Peanut shells	
Raffia	Fabric scraps	Old keys	
Tinfoil	Film containers	Vinyl	
Lace	Leaves		
Felt	Jar lids		
Pompons	Milk cartons		
Popsicle sticks	Newspaper		
Yarn	Oatmeal		
Ribbon	Containers		
Markers	Pill containers		
Crayons	Pinecones	Balsa wood	String
Colored pencils	Batting	Indian corn	Clock hands
Gumdrops	<u>Acorns</u>	Safety glasses	Leather
Marbles	Sand	Thumbtacks	Appliqués
Rhinestones	Needle	Brushes	Nail polish
Sequins	Thread	Glass	Rulers
Hair swatches	<u>Stencils</u>	Screens	Cat whiskers
<u>Paint</u>	Rocks and pebbles	Paper cutter	Wax
Seashells	Steel wool	Dyes	Styrofoam balls
Seeds	Hairnets	Measuring tape	Sticks

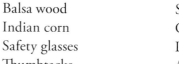

SCRAMBLER

```
Y R X Q F E A T H E R S O P
U N D K R F T L O S M B O X
W Z N O T B D X G U W L A G
G M Y E V U S N Y R Z M K I
V T R P L C I F Q O B T H B
M B C G D V H J T K Y A S N
T V E L A S T I C S U F D K
Y Q R H U K U L O V M X A W
H F S J I U D P L W V B E Q
D A T S C L A C O R N S B C
A I T M I W L U R Y Z I Q A
W R E F O E P Z E G L A U I
F K C X W K S G D P C U J D
Z S L U I C E K T I N C A N
J P T O R U D Q A X V Y U G
H O G L E T G B P A I N T I
W N Z U B M W J E F Q C H J
S G K D G A B O V K Y R E D
U E R L J U E C D E M X G Y
F S U R M K V D P O I N H E
J K N S T E N C I L S W F S
```

acknowledgements

E ven though my name is on the cover of this book it was a group effort. Of course, I could have put the whole group on the cover along with me, but then I would be acknowledging people in a much more prominent place than the little-read "acknowledgments" page, and I'm not sure how that benefits me. What I am sure about is that trying to juggle a husband and a family is difficult when one is trying to write a book. I wish I had those distractions. Maybe I'll get a husband and some children when I write my next book, but I couldn't imagine doing another book without my team. They are tireless, selfless, and magnificently creative. I have found there is a difference between motivation and inspiration: this book was created by highly motivated and talented people who are listed below, and most of the inspiration came from the cannabis plant and from watching my generous and brilliant underpaid workers slave away.

Photography by **Jason Frank Rothenberg**
Embroidery art by **Megan Whitmarsh**
Costumes by **Adam Selman**
Illustrations by **Justin Theroux**
Book design by **Lenny Naar**

GUEST STARS

Lilian Todd—paper cutouts, paper presidents
Cindy Sherman—balloon flowers
Frank Proto—sausage information and recipes
Adam Ottavi Schiesl—Worm Bin information
Julie Le—cake balls
Cathy Camper—seed art of James Brown
Lauren Smith—stuffed animals, Mexican Sugar Skulls, Felt Fruit of Our Labor Pins, walnut mouse
Conn Brattain—coconut masks, Coconut Face Necklace, Coconut Face Pin, Coconut Chip Necklace and Earrings, coconut votive candle holder, Bamboo Bone Necklace and Earrings, Rock Rings, ribbons, Pompon Golf Club Covers
Leslie Hall—Leslie's Rug

Philip Crangi—tassels, Smelly Balsam Sack, Sentimental Hair Earrings
Gretchen Sedaris—Nut Wreaths, leaf paintings, bark toiletries set, Penny Bookmark, googly-eyed Nutly clan, glitter clothespins
Kate Fenker—knitted sausages, miniature sweater
Lacy Boyles—knitted vest, knitted candle holders, pompon slippers
Lucia Stern—rattle boxes
Linda Oldham—Beaded Spiderweb
L. J. Grassy—votives, headstones
Megan Whitmarsh—puffy prescription bottle, embroidered ring size chart, handmade googly eyes
Ann McCullen—Tea Cozy Kitten
Todd Oldham—Tinfoil Bracelet
CoCo's Confections—decorative cookies

ALSO...

Jenna Jones—handwritten recipe cards

Mel Ottenberg—scrap stamp box, Secret Treasure Box

Tom Bonauro—comet image print

Callie Thorne—"Green Stamps" poem, Smelly Oil recipe

Tony Longoria—greasy box with bead top, tape-decorated boxes

Dean Sawyer—cardboard floral hang-up, Crock Pot Butter

Daniel Griffin—Hobo Fire in a Can, Planetarium, Matchstick Cross, teenager box, prison pencil case

Brock Shorno—Cardboard Indoor Rabbit Dwelling, wooden bats

Teri Lyn Pugliese—Lil' Hot Foot Fire Starter

Franco Vigliarolo—Clothespin Jesus

Anne Vigliarolo—Crock-Pot recipes

Nancy Lenehan—Knitted Fingerless Gloves

Billy Erb—thumbtack initials, Hair Lamp

Kathy Cano-Murillo—Glitter Box and Paper Flowers

Zaldy—Wheelchair Backpack

Mary Cotter—rabbit information

Jill Watson—nurse (disorder help)

Mary Adams—Cotton Ball Heating Pad Cover

Madelyn Sedaris—googly-eyed acorns in theater box

Paul Sedaris—owl drawing, Googly-Eyed Clamshell, Crab Claw Roach Clip

Olaf E. Coerper—Book Covers

Jonathan Kopita—Book Covers

Mildred Jasper—"Granny"-stenciled pillowcases

Katie Richardson—Elliot's Cilantro Treats

Stephen Colbert—china plate piece pin

Carlos Zepeda—Pin Tower Cushion

Erika Harada—stitching on cork typewriter

Carlis Conner—pompons on cover

Shannon Thompson—Brown Sugar and Lavender Body Scrub

Bestar Mujaj, Shelby Scudder, Molly Donato, Helen Ann Lally, Kouta, Amber Hodgson, Andy Cohen, Frank Dinello, Janet West, Sarah Fargo, Lou Sedaris, Caitlin Bristol, Justin Space, Hugh Hamrick, Marshall Wyatt, Mark Ibold, David Cohn, Richard "Woofie" Fox, Ann Dinello, Cindy Selman, Antonia Xereas, Michael Ingulli, Sonia Gallo, Sheila Harris, Eric Russell, Brian Sawyer, Jocelyn, Amy Einhorn, Neil Patrick Harris.

MY SIMPLE TIMES CRAFTERS AND CONTRIBUTORS TEAM

For their endless contributions to the book...

Olivia Mori, Nathaniel Baker Overstreet (also for Woodchuck portraits), Laren Leblanc (also costume assistant), Hillary Moore, Jennifer McCullen, Todd Oldham, Vicki Farrell (also for lettering on the cover and title page), Debbie Lelievre (also for special effects makeup, as well as all character makeup, except for the Crafting for Jesus chapter), Paul Dinello, Adam Selman

THANK YOU TO THE PEOPLE AT HACHETTE...

Jamie Raab, Anne Twomey, Barbara Brown, Evan Boorstyn, Lizzy Kornblit, Emily Griffin, Sara Weiss, Tom Whatley, Antoinette Marotta, Tareth Mitch, Leah Tracosas, Dylan Hoke, Renée Gelman, Anthony Goff, Michele McGonigle, Justine Gardner, Mark Kondracki

AND FROM WME I WOULD LIKE TO THANK...

Tracy Fisher, Eric Zohn, Amy Hasselbeck, Pauline Post

Simple Times

INDEX

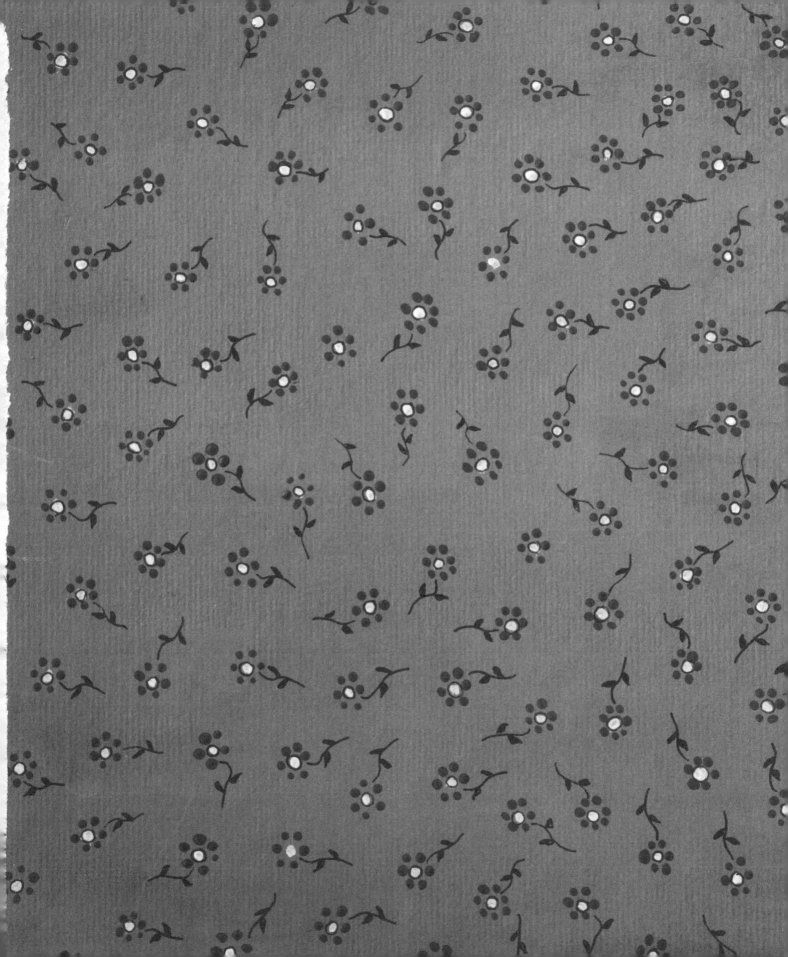